I AM transformed

40 DAYS TO UNLEASH THE POWER OF

YOUR GOD-GIVEN IDENTITY

SONS & DAUGHTERS

Revell

a division of Baker Publishing Group
Grand Rapids, Michigan

© 2022 by Messenger International

Published by Revell
a division of Baker Publishing Group
PO Box 6287, Grand Rapids, MI 49516-6287
www.revellbooks.com

Printed in the United States of America

Library of Congress Cataloging-in-Publication Data
Names: Sons & Daughters (Colorado Springs, Colo.) author.
Title: I am transformed : 40 days to unleash the power of your God-given identity / Sons & Daughters.
Description: Grand Rapids, MI : Revell, a division of Baker Publishing Group, [2022]
Identifiers: LCCN 2022006577 | ISBN 9780800737696 (paperback) | ISBN 9781493438754 (ebook)
Subjects: LCSH: Identity (Psychology)—Religious aspects—Christianity—Miscellanea. | Young adults—Religious life—Miscellanea.
Classification: LCC BV4509.5 .S675 2022 | DDC 155.2—dc23/eng/20220328
LC record available at https://lccn.loc.gov/2022006577

Scripture quotations are from THE HOLY BIBLE, NEW INTERNATIONAL VERSION®, NIV® Copyright © 1973, 1978, 1984, 2011 by Biblica, Inc.® Used by permission. All rights reserved worldwide.

Sons & Daughters is represented by the literary agency of The Fedd Agency.

Baker Publishing Group publications use paper produced from sustainable forestry practices and post-consumer waste whenever possible.

22 23 24 25 26 27 28   7 6 5 4 3 2 1

To the sons and daughters who've paved the way,
the ones embracing the adventure today,
and those who will lead one day.

CONTENTS

HOW TO USE THIS BOOK

HAVE YOU EVER NOTICED pets and their owners who look way too much alike? Like, it's borderline creepy? Or married couples who over the years have begun to look more and more the same? Or friend groups who dress, talk, and even laugh alike, even though they'd all probably deny it?

It's not a bad thing to look like someone you love or admire. In fact, it's human nature.

We do the same thing with God, actually. The more time we spend with him, the more we live like him and love like him. The goal of this forty-day devotional experience is based on that idea. Each day, we'll look at a unique truth about God and a corresponding truth about ourselves.

That order is important: first God, then us. Too often we get this backward. We think we must take the lead and let God do his work in our wake. We believe it's up to us to impress God, convince God, or even manipulate God by polishing our lives to perfection.

Really, we just need to *reflect* God.

We were created in his image, after all. It's only natural that we should resemble him. The more we understand who he is, the more his image begins to shine in us, and the more we become like him in our day-to-day lives. We start by looking at him, and we end up looking like him as we surrender and let his goodness and greatness transform us from the inside out.

Remember, God already loves us. He's our Father, our friend, our Lord, and our biggest fan. Our relationship with him is not in danger. He's not stressing out about our accomplishments or our maturity level or our marital status or our career progress or any of the other things that so often puncture our self-esteem. Instead, he is inviting us to follow him, to learn from him, and to become like him.

Again, that's the heart behind this interactive devotional, which consists of forty short entries loosely organized under what we call our I Am Covenant. You might want to read through the devotional over forty days or you might prefer to cover one section per week for seven weeks, whichever works best for you. Each devotional is broken up into these four sections.

REST

Before you jump in to the main part of the devotional, we encourage you to take two full minutes (or more) to settle your mind and emotions. This might be harder than you expect. It's a lot easier to keep your mind busy than it is to keep it calm. But calm is what you need.

Consider setting a timer so you don't rush too quickly through this section. Take a moment to read the introductory text, then simply breathe. Pay attention to what you are feeling. Maybe God wants to speak into some of those areas today. If so, that's his role. Yours is to trust, to rest, to wait, to obey.

Once your thoughts and heart are settled, move on to the Read portion.

READ

In this section we look at two things: a quality or trait of God and a parallel application in our own lives. We look at who God is and how his nature is reflected in us.

The goal of this section isn't to be overly complicated, but it's not intended to offer cliché or superficial answers either. We will look at questions we all face, and we will ask what God's nature and image mean for us on an intensely practical level.

The truths we examine are all based on Scripture, and we've included references within the text. If you'd like to dive deeper into any topic, there are also two or three passages for additional thought included at the end of each reading.

REFLECT

Each devotional includes three questions to help you reflect on and apply what you've just read. These are completely personal, so there's no answer key. They are simply starting points for self-evaluation.

If you are reading this devotional on your own, you might want to write the answers in this book or in a separate journal. If you are reading this with a group and would prefer to discuss them aloud, these questions can lead to deep, healthy conversations.

RESPOND

We've left space at the end of each devotional for hands-on interaction with the topic. Whether you consider yourself artistic or not, we invite you to take a few moments to express what you're feeling in some creative, personal way.

That might be through poetry, an outline, brainstorming, a sketch, song lyrics, abstract art, doodles, a metaphor, creative writing, or anything else that fits who you are and how you think.

Have fun with this section! It is yours to do with as you please, to express yourself freely. It just might become your favorite part of the day.

And . . . that's it! You're ready to begin.

PART 1
i am holy

I AM HOLY, SO I STAND OUT FROM THE CROWD. I recognize that holiness is so much more than "following the rules." Holiness is not an attempt to just be good enough. Rather, it's my journey of embracing everything my Father has for me. A journey into the beauty, wonder, and majesty of what it is to be a child of God and share in his nature. It's his nature within that makes me stand out. God's holiness transforms every area of my life. And because of his Spirit and grace, I can be holy—in thought, word, and deed. To be holy is to be whole. To be holy is to be his. I am holy, so I stand out from the crowd.

DAY 1

GOD IS PERFECT,
so i am growing

REST

As you get started today, take two minutes to simply be still. Let the stress and hurry and noise of life fade into the background as your spirit comes alive.

Breathe in, breathe out, breathe in again. Focus on exchanging stress for peace, shame for confidence, fear for courage.

When you are finished, whisper to yourself, *I am loved. I am holy. I am complete. I am enough.*

READ

What Perfect Really Means   Is there anything in your life that has to be perfect, or else you start to go a little crazy? Maybe you can't stand clutter around the house. Or everything on your desk needs to be exactly in its place before you can concentrate. Or you try on seventeen different clothing combinations every morning until your outfit is a flawless work of art.

We are all perfectionists in at least a few areas. And in other areas . . . not so much. You can probably think of some things you don't care that much about so you don't try too hard to perfect them.

That's normal. The problem is when the things you don't care about are precisely the things your roommate or spouse obsesses over. Or vice versa. At that point, either someone has to change or sparks will fly. Perfection and chaos can't coexist, right?

Wrong.

Just look at God, then look at us. God is perfect. In *every* way, not just a few. We are far from perfect. And yet he doesn't roll his eyes at us while dropping passive-aggressive, semi-snarky comments about the dishes we left in the sink, metaphorically speaking.

You see, we tend to think of perfection as just being free from sin, error, or weakness. The issue is that we're works in progress. We make mistakes. We suffer lack. We struggle with weakness. So if "perfect" means never messing up, we might as well give up now. We're set for failure.

In the Bible, though, the term *perfect* refers to the idea of becoming complete. It alludes to maturity, wholeness, or fullness. We often see this term used to encourage growth in a variety of areas.

For example, on one occasion, Jesus was teaching about loving everyone, even our enemies. He instructed his listeners to share his wide, expansive, unconditional love with all people, including their enemies. Then he pointed to how God "causes his sun to rise on the evil and the good, and sends rain on the righteous and the unrighteous" (Matt. 5:45). A few verses later he concluded with this summary: "Be perfect, therefore, as your heavenly Father is perfect" (v. 48).

Do you see the connection in this passage between becoming better at *love* and becoming more *perfect*? When Jesus said "be perfect," he wasn't commanding us to meet an impossible moral standard of some obsessive, perfectionistic deity. Rather, he was challenging us to become as complete in our love as God is in his. If we want to be like him, we need to have a diverse, wide, inclusive, open-armed love, even for those who don't like us or who go out of their way to oppose us.

But love is just one of God's qualities. He is complete in every sense. He is perfectly wise, strong, good, true, faithful, kind, pure, and generous. He lacks nothing and has everything. As children of God who are made in his image, we are called to become complete or whole, to grow in holiness.

In a spiritual sense, we are already complete. That's an important truth to keep in mind, particularly when the process of personal growth is slower than we'd like. In Christ, we are children of God: loved, approved, and accepted by him. Jesus is our advocate, so we have nothing to fear and nothing to prove.

But our journey toward perfection is a work in progress. That's obvious, right? We all have room to grow. Not because we are trying to avoid disappointing a perfectionistic God, but because we believe we can be as complete and whole as he created us to be. Perfection is a process to embrace, not a goal to reach.

The good news is God is committed to that growth process. In fact, it was *his* idea. That's why Paul wrote, "He who began a good work in you will carry it on to completion until the day of Christ Jesus" (Phil. 1:6).

What areas are you lacking in today? Where would you like to grow? What part of your inner or outer world needs to be made whole? Today, as you pray, express those things to God, and let his perfection encourage you toward growth.

For further thought, read James 1:2–4 and 2 Peter 1:5–8.

REFLECT

1. Is it hard to believe that you are already enough in God's eyes? Why or why not?

2. In what areas would you like to grow and become more complete?

3. What is the "good work" that God began in you (Phil. 1:6)? What are some specific ways he might "carry it on to completion"?

respond

During your devotional time, use this space to creatively express what the concept of growing and becoming whole means to you. For example, you might jot down your thoughts about God's perfection, draw something that illustrates how you feel on this journey, or write a poem about who you are becoming.

GOD IS WISE,
so i am teachable

REST

Take a moment to focus your thoughts on God. There is no rush, no hurry, no better place to be.

Mentally release into God's hands anything negative or painful that you are feeling. Cast your cares on him, for he cares for you.

Then tell yourself, *I am safe and loved. I am holy and whole. I am wise and teachable.*

READ

You Might Be Wrong   One of the best things about social media is that it gives everyone a platform to express their opinion about anything and everything. Right? It's awesome.

Except when it's not.

Everybody is entitled to their opinion, but sometimes those opinions can get a little . . . intense. We've all seen more than a few narrow-minded posts, spiteful comments, and ignorant replies. They get our blood boiling and our brains spinning. *How can someone possibly think that?*

Responding is useless. We know that. But the temptation is too much to resist sometimes. After all, what if our carefully crafted, semi-sarcastic response is exactly what that person needs to finally understand the point they seem to be missing?

So, we compose our thoughts, type our comeback, and hit Send. It doesn't help, of course. But at least we feel a bit better after blowing off steam. Until they reply, anyway. Then the crazy cycle continues.

We all have opinions, and that's a beautiful thing. It really is.

Even when those opinions clash and even when they are not expressed with wisdom or tact, at least we have the capacity to reason, to debate, and to grow. And that's a gift from God. He wants us to learn, and he often uses other fallible human beings to challenge or adjust our assumptions.

The problem arises when we forget that our opinion is simply that: it's ours, and it's an opinion. *Ours* means it's personal. It's a belief we stand by and a mindset we hold to. Other people can and should have their own opinions, and we need to respect each other enough to walk in love even when we strongly disagree.

Opinion means it's not fact. This is hard to accept because we all want to be certain about what we believe. We assume that if we study, reason, and learn enough about a particular topic, we will arrive at the truth. Then we will never have to study or reason or learn again.

Let's be honest though. We are finite, fallible, fickle human beings. We don't know everything, because we're not God. Even the truths we think we know must be held with an open hand because *we might be wrong*.

That shouldn't discourage us—but it should humble us. Even more than that, it should point us to the One who does have absolute truth.

God doesn't deal in opinions, guesses, estimates, or assumptions. He never has to change his mind or backtrack on his statements, because he's never wrong. He is the ultimate source of knowledge and understanding.

God doesn't keep his wisdom to himself though. He shares it with us. James wrote, "If any of you lacks wisdom, you should ask God, who gives generously to all without finding fault, and it will be given to you" (1:5). And even Solomon said, "The LORD gives wisdom; from his mouth come knowledge and understanding" (Prov. 2:6).

That doesn't necessarily mean God will give you the perfect comeback for that online debate, but it does mean he will help you live wisely and well. If you are willing to learn, he will show you how to make good decisions, how to handle your money, how to love people better, how to find inner peace, how to establish good habits, and more.

That wisdom rarely comes in the form of an audible voice from heaven. God typically uses less dramatic channels of communication to shape us, including—as we noted above—humans with opinions that don't line up with ours. He also uses the Bible, which is the best and most objective source of his wisdom. And along with that, God's Spirit (the spirit of wisdom) guides us into all truth as we collect experiences, counsel, logic, common sense, and more. God is committed to our growth, and he uses whatever means necessary to speak to our hearts and minds if we take the time to listen.

So, what is your role in this process? First, *be teachable*. That means holding your opinions with an open hand, allowing God to lead you, and being willing to change your mind. Second, *seek wisdom*. This is your responsibility, not God's. Personal growth requires hard work and a good dose of humility. You'll get out of the growth process what you are willing to put into it. Third, *respond quickly*. It's not enough to just know what's right—you also need to put your understanding into practice by making real changes. And finally, *keep growing*. Learning comes in stages. Just because you learned something today doesn't mean you won't need to learn it again tomorrow.

How about you? Where do you need God's wisdom today? Choose to be open, teachable, and humble. Then get ready. Answers will come.

For further thought, read Proverbs 4:1–9 and James 3:13–18.

REFLECT

1. How would you define *wisdom*?

2. Is it easy or hard for you to change your mind? Why is that?

3. If you could learn about any topic or grow in any area, what would it be? Why?

respond

Think about God's vast wisdom and imagine yourself as a continual learner, receiving from him. What does it mean to you that God knows everything? That you are always growing? That God's truth brings so much life and freedom? Use the space provided to describe or illustrate these truths in whatever creative way feels best to you.

GOD IS UNCHANGING,
so i am consistent

REST

There are a lot of things you don't know and a lot of things you can't control. Think about that for a moment and make peace with it.

Then let it go.

Let go of expectations. Let go of the illusion of control. Let go of the tyranny of perfection. Let go of the labels and the limits that hold you back. Take a couple of minutes to be fully present, fully you. Finish by whispering, *I am me, I am here, and I matter.*

READ

Taking Up Space   Have you ever been stood up by someone? It's not a great feeling. Nobody wants to be ignored, forgotten, or snubbed, and none of us like to have our time wasted.

There are exceptions, of course. If your dentist accidentally double-booked herself and stood you up for a root canal, you probably wouldn't be all that upset. If an IRS auditor got lost trying to find your office and instead decided to cancel the audit he had planned, you'd call it God's divine intervention.

But for the most part, standing someone up is not okay. We've all been there, and we've probably all done it to others. Hopefully it wasn't on purpose, but let's be real—we make mistakes. We agree to help somebody move and forget to show up. We set a date to hang out with a friend and then plan a trip out of town. We promise to go to our boss's party, knowing we will probably find an excuse to cancel at the last minute.

God, on the other hand, has never stood anyone up, and he never will. He doesn't forget to write things down in his calendar. He doesn't overbook himself. He doesn't bail at the last minute. He doesn't ignore us, forget us, or snub us. The prophet Balaam said this about God:

> God is not human, that he should lie,
>   not a human being, that he should change his mind.
> Does he speak and then not act?
>   Does he promise and not fulfill? (Num. 23:19)

In the story that verse is taken from, God had promised to bless Israel, but an enemy king was trying to convince Balaam to curse Israel instead. The king thought Balaam had some special power to manipulate his deity into doing whatever he wanted. Balaam made it clear to the king that nobody tells God what to do. If God had decided to bless his people, no king or prophet or army was going to get in his way. Why? Because God wouldn't go back on his word. Ever.

God has also promised to bless you. And like the story of Balaam and Israel, he's not going to change his mind. Chances are you don't have a literal human enemy trying to bribe prophets to curse you. That would be weird. But maybe you have a voice in your head, trying to speak evil over you. Perhaps a mocking whisper echoes inside your mind, insisting you aren't enough, your failures are too great, your strength is too small.

Rather than letting that voice convince you that your mistakes have torpedoed your future, turn to God. Let his unchanging, unwavering, un-alterable Word build your faith. God is the only one who is never gonna give you up, never gonna let you down (no offense, Rick Astley). In all seriousness, though, God really won't let you down. He doesn't change his mind, his Word, his will, or his ways. You can always count on him. As the author of Hebrews famously wrote, "Jesus Christ is the same yesterday and today and forever" (13:8). Don't let the ups and downs of life convince you otherwise.

You do have a role to play in all this, of course. God will show up for you, but you have to show up for *life*. You were created in the image of a faithful God, and you are called to be faithful. Not just in your appointments or your social calendar, but in who you are and how you live.

That means taking up the space God called you to fill. It means showing up, standing up, rising up, speaking up. Do your best to be consistent and faithful, day in and day out.

God doesn't ask you to be perfect, but he does ask you to be consistent. It's not about never failing or falling. Consistency is simply about showing up over and over. And if you do fall down, it's about getting back up.

How can you show up for life today? How can you show up for others? For God? You can't know everything or control everything, but you can strive for consistency in what you do. And in the long run, that will take you where you want to go.

For further thought, read Psalm 103:13–18 and James 1:17.

REFLECT

1. Have you ever felt let down by God? How did you deal with that?

2. Is it hard for you to believe that you matter? Why or why not?

3. What are some areas where you could improve at showing up or being consistent?

respond

Write or draw something in the space below that is inspired by the unchanging, always-faithful reality of God. How could you describe or illustrate these characteristics? Is there a symbol, a picture, or a metaphor that explains how you feel?

DAY 4

GOD IS ONE,
so i am whole

REST

God is love. Imagine yourself enveloped by love—safe and warm, comforted and comfortable. Visualize yourself becoming one with God, one with love. Let him fill any cracks in your heart, your mind, or your emotions. Let him make you whole.

Now, take a minute to simply be still. You don't have to do anything or say anything. Just rest in his love for as long as you need to.

When you are ready, repeat to yourself, *I am complete. I am whole. I am healthy. I am holy.*

READ

How to Be Yourself   "I'm just not myself today."

It's probably safe to say we've all said something like that at some point. Most likely as an apology of sorts, an explanation of why we've been acting a bit off.

Maybe you snapped at your roommate because they forgot to take out the garbage. Or you were distracted when your boss was trying to explain something. Or you felt frustrated with your significant other about some dumb thing that normally wouldn't matter.

When you realized that the problem was you, not the world around you, you admitted with a tinge of embarrassment, "I'm just not feeling like myself." Then you hopefully got a coffee or took a nap or ate lunch or scheduled a vacation or did something else to become "yourself" again. To pull back into alignment the emotions, thoughts, or health issues that were disordered.

Sometimes this fragmentation goes deeper than a momentary lapse of manners. It could be a lifestyle. You might find yourself playing a part, trying to meet expectations, smiling on the outside but struggling on the inside. Over time, that becomes exhausting. You realize there is a disconnect between who people think you are and who you really are, between who you are and who you want to be, or how you are acting and what you truly value.

The answer to finding wholeness depends on where your fragmentation comes from. There is no quick fix to becoming the same person on the inside and the outside, to being consistent in every situation. A good way to start, though, is by drawing near to God.

Wholeness begins with God. Why? Because he is whole. He is not fractured or fragmented. God is congruent and complete, unchanging and unchangeable. He is holy. He doesn't alter his behavior out of fear of rejection. His emotions don't change because he missed breakfast. No matter what, God acts in accordance with who he is.

And who he is, is love.

God's oneness and God's love are connected. Think about it. God is always true to love. He cannot act outside of love because love is who he is. His pure, unselfish love defines everything he does. God is guided by love, committed to love, and motivated by love.

Notice how the apostle John linked God's oneness to his love:

> This is how we know that we live in him and he in us: He has given us of his Spirit. And we have seen and testify that the Father has sent his Son to be the Savior of the world. If anyone acknowledges that Jesus is the Son of God, God lives in them and they in God. And so we know and rely on the love God has for us.
>
> God is love. Whoever lives in love lives in God, and God in them. (1 John 4:13–16)

John mentioned the Spirit, the Father, and the Son, all in the context of love. He was showing us how the Trinity, or the three-person nature of God, is united in love and how that love unites us to God. John went on to say that love is "made complete" in us, and divine love drives out fear and makes us "perfect in love" (vv. 17–18).

Love can mean different things to different people, but God's oneness is defined by holy love, and he completes us in that love. Selfishness has no place in God's holiness, so his love always brings out the best in us.

What does that mean for you? When you aren't feeling yourself (or when you are trying to figure out who "yourself" even is), love is the best place to turn. A lifestyle characterized by love will always be more whole, more authentic, and more congruent than a lifestyle characterized by selfishness or fear. It is a holy life.

The same love that makes God so authentic can bring wholeness to you. Not just when your roommate is getting on your nerves or your kids are making you question your sanity but also when you are struggling to figure out who you are or why God put you on this planet in the first place. In those confusing, faltering moments, let God's love give you purpose. Let it define you, direct you, unite you.

How does love heal the fractures and close the fissures of the soul? In other words, how does God's holiness make us whole? In many ways. By affirming who you are right now, to start with. By aligning your priorities and guiding your decisions. By giving you courage to lay down your old sense of self so you can live in the reality of who you truly are.

If you find yourself a little scattered or fractured today, try leaning into God's love. Let his consistency make you whole. Let his mercy give you peace. Let his faithfulness pull the pieces of your life back into alignment.

You don't have to play a part. You don't have to be tossed and turned, pushed and pulled, swayed and strained and stressed by the forces around you.

Be filled with holy love, and you'll be wholly and authentically *you*.

For further thought, read John 15:1–9 and Ephesians 2:10.

REFLECT

1. Are there areas of your life—thoughts, emotions, goals, relationships —where you find yourself struggling to "be yourself"? What are they?

2. Do you see holiness as wholeness? Why or why not?

3. Does becoming more authentic mean becoming more selfish and self-centered, or more generous? Why?

What does it mean to you to be congruent, complete, authentic? Use the space below to illustrate God's wholeness, your own wholeness, or both. Feel free to use words, doodles, poetry, a self-portrait, abstract art, or anything else that gets your thoughts and feelings onto paper.

GOD IS SINLESS,
so i am pure

REST

Quiet your thoughts and bring your focus to God. Maybe it's morning right now and your day is still ahead of you, or it's evening and you're finally able to relax, or maybe it's somewhere in between. Regardless, block out the busyness of the day and be still.

Breathe slowly, rhythmically, deliberately. After a couple of minutes of stillness, whisper to God, *I am safe in your presence. I trust you. I need you. Being with you is what matters most.*

READ

Help More, Harm Less   Have you ever been at a restaurant, laughing and distracted with friends, and taken a drink of whatever you had in your glass, only to realize that you just swallowed a UFO—an unidentified floating object?

Your imagination runs wild. What was that? Was it a bug? If a bug, what kind? Was it alive? Did it have wings? Did it have a family? Did it have dreams?

Just as you begin to hyperventilate, you realize—or you decide to believe, for the sake of your sanity—that it must have been a sliver of ice, nearly melted, harmless, and definitely not alive.

There are few things more shocking than expecting to ingest one thing and realizing too late that it was mixed with something else. We want what goes into our mouths and stomachs to be pure, clean, and unaccompanied by foreign objects. Particularly objects with legs and wings.

The word *pure* describes something that is completely itself, unmixed with anything else, free from harmful contaminants. The purity of a thing adds to its effectiveness, whereas contamination reduces that effectiveness. Pure water is deeply refreshing, for example. Pure joy is euphoric. Pure love is world changing.

God is absolutely pure. He has no mixture of contaminants, no harmful characteristics, no hidden danger, no poisonous components. Another way of describing him is *sinless*. Sin is, by definition, anything contrary to God's nature. Sin is harmful and damaging, which means it cannot exist in a God who is completely holy or pure.

Because we were created in God's image, we are also called to be pure, holy, sinless. Without mixture or contaminants. Free of unidentified floating objects, in other words. The author of Hebrews wrote, "Make every effort to live in peace with everyone and to be holy; without holiness no one will see the Lord" (12:14).

Remember, though, that purity was never meant to be a scorecard. We too easily turn purity into an end in itself. It becomes a proof of our faith, a sign of our commitment, a badge of our moral superiority when compared to those around us. Of course, when we fail, our lack of purity becomes a source of shame and guilt. Neither one of those responses, arrogance or shame, is helpful to anybody.

Think about what purity means: to be free of harmful contaminants. The focus of purity should not be on the thing that is pure, but on the *reason* it is pure. For example, it doesn't matter how pure a bottle of water is if nobody drinks it. Who cares how pure water on a shelf is? The point of water is to refresh, hydrate, and satisfy. The purer it is when somebody drinks it, the better it accomplishes that purpose.

Purity has a purpose, but that purpose is not bragging rights. The purpose is to *help more* and *harm less*. It's to be a blessing to ourselves, our families, our friends, and others. Sin is inherently damaging, so it interferes with that purpose. That's why we reject it. Paul told Timothy, "Flee the evil desires of youth and pursue righteousness, faith, love and peace, along with those who call on the Lord out of a pure heart" (2 Tim. 2:22). The goal is to put aside what harms us and others and embrace what is pure and helpful.

Purity divorced from purpose is too easily weaponized. When love is not the motivation to abstain from sin, we subconsciously use it to control, reject, shame, or label. But that use of purity misses the point entirely.

Think about God. His purity is a blessing to us, not a weapon used against us. He exercises love, joy, peace, patience, goodness, mercy, faithfulness, and forgiveness in his dealings with us, and those qualities have transformed our lives. His purity is our blessing.

God asks us to embody those same qualities. Why? Not to claim the moral high ground over someone else. Not because we are getting graded on our sanctity. Not because our salvation hangs in the balance. Not because purity is an end in itself. Rather, because the purer something is, the better it is at fulfilling its purpose.

That includes us. The purer we are in our love, our motives, our thoughts, and our actions, the better we will be at this crazy venture called life. That's why God roots out whatever gets in the way: pride, anger, selfishness, fear, lust, greed, revenge, violence, and oppression. When those things are mixed in with who we are or how we act, they harm us and those around us. When they are removed, we are free to be blessed and to be a blessing.

So in your pursuit of holiness, don't focus primarily on yourself. Remember, you are created in the image of a pure God, and your holiness is a reflection of him, not something you can accomplish in your own strength. God already loves you, accepts you, forgives you, and chooses you. Now he calls you to reflect him.

Embrace purity, but for the right reason: to become the best version of yourself possible, to help the most people, to enjoy life to the fullest, and to glorify your Father in heaven.

Also, always look at your drink before taking a sip.

For further thought, read Genesis 12:2–3 and Romans 6:15–23.

REFLECT

1. How would you define *sin*? Why do you think God tells us to avoid sin and pursue holiness?

2. Have you ever been harmed by an overemphasis on purity? How was that understanding of purity flawed?

3. What areas of your life might need a bit of purifying? What benefits do you think you would see from being purer in those areas?

respond

Use the space provided to illustrate what *pure* means to you. You might want to think about the benefits of purity or the holiness of God. You might even want to push back somehow against the false stereotypes of shame and guilt that are often attached to purity. Purity is freedom, after all, and blessing. How could you describe or illustrate that in your own way?

DAY 6

GOD IS TRUTH,
so i am free

REST

Before you begin, take a moment to evaluate yourself. Is anything causing you fear? Stress? Anger? Confusion? Pain?

Don't try to solve those problems right now. Instead, release them to God. Cast your cares on him. Replace the worries and stressors with the simple freedom found in Jesus.

Say to yourself, *God cares for me, and he knows my needs. I am at peace. I am at rest. I am free.*

READ

What Really Sets You Free   What did you *really* learn in high school? That is, what were the lessons or truths that carried over into real life?

For most of us, the awkward truth is that the intricacies of precalculus will be forgotten about sixty seconds after we graduate. The atomic number of plutonium, the main exports of Liechtenstein, and the dates of the Paleozoic Era tend to get stashed away in the darkest, dustiest recesses of the mind, never to be seen or heard from again.

Until you have kids. And your kids have homework. Then suddenly you find yourself rummaging around in those dusty recesses, trying to piece together what you forgot many years ago.

Just because your brain jettisoned some of the names and places and dates and formulas doesn't mean school was a waste though. Grade school—like every stage of life—teaches you truths that include facts and data but go far beyond them.

What you *really* learned in school was critical thinking, teamwork, social skills, work ethic, creativity, memorization techniques, discipline, logic, and much more. Those are the skills that will carry you through life, long after the Pythagorean theorem and the quadratic equation have faded into oblivion.

Truth is more than facts and data. Truth is what is real. It is what works, what matters, what stands the test of time.

The book of Proverbs has a lot to say about this topic. Words like *wisdom*, *understanding, knowledge, insight*, and *discernment* appear hundreds of times. The central theme of the book is the importance of growing in our knowledge of truth and our ability to apply it.

In the New Testament, Paul told the Colossians,

> For this reason, since the day we heard about you, we have not stopped praying for you. We continually ask God to fill you with the knowledge of his will through all the wisdom and understanding that the Spirit gives, so that you may live a life worthy of the Lord and please him in every way: bearing fruit in every good work, growing in the knowledge of God. (1:9–10)

Notice how Paul desired that they would both know the truth *and* grow into the truth.

Clearly truth is important to God. Why? Does God obsess over trivia and minutiae? Does he care about random facts, obscure formulas, and the difference between a participle and a gerund? Does our entrance into heaven depend on our ability to work out a proof in geometry?

That would be terrifying.

God does care about details, but truth is not about filling our heads with facts. According to Jesus, truth brings *freedom*. He told his followers, "Then you will know the truth, and the truth will set you free" (John 8:32).

The point of truth is not to know more, but to live better in obedience to God. It is to accomplish more, to make fewer mistakes, to work more effectively, to love people more. Error wastes our time and energy, but truth gives us freedom. It enables us to live in a sustainable, healthy, holy way.

That's why Paul told the Corinthian church, "We know that 'We all possess knowledge.' But knowledge puffs up while love builds up" (1 Cor. 8:1). He was reminding them that the point of knowledge is to become better human beings, not walking encyclopedias.

Truth is always practical. And truth always leads to freedom.

Finding truth is a lifelong pursuit. That means opening your heart and mind to God in prayer. It means studying the Bible and increasing in your knowledge of Scripture. It means paying attention in life and growing from both failure and success. It means honoring those who've gone before you. And it means pursuing education, learning, and wisdom.

What areas of your life need truth today? God is the source of that truth, and he wants to share it with you.

For further thought, read John 1:17; 4:24; 8:32–47.

REFLECT

1. What is your favorite way to learn something new?

2. In what areas have you found greater freedom or effectiveness through growing in truth?

3. Looking toward the future, in what topics or areas would you like to grow in wisdom and understanding?

respond

Think about the concepts of truth and freedom. What do those ideas mean? How have they changed you? How could you describe them? Use the space below to illustrate what truth and freedom look like for you.

PART 2

i am righteous

I AM RIGHTEOUS, SO I FIGHT FOR JUSTICE. Righteousness is an intrinsic part of my identity in Christ. Christ's blood has given me new life, so I belong in the family of God. And because I am found within, I fight for those without. My world is bigger than myself, so I live free from the tyranny of self-centeredness. And it's in the beauty of selflessness that I find the perspective to lay down my life, look up, and follow in the footsteps of Jesus—my big brother—the only person who got this whole humanity thing right. I am righteous, so I fight for justice.

GOD IS JUST,
so i am forgiven

REST

Take a full two minutes to simply be still. You don't need to say anything or pray anything. Just wait. Calm your mind.

Surrender any guilt or shame. Maybe you don't feel like you're enough. Maybe you are disappointed in yourself for some reason. Let God take those deficiencies, those doubts.

When you are finished, whisper to yourself, *I am loved. I am accepted. I am forgiven.*

READ

Pursued by Justice From police chases to courtroom dramas to Wild West shootouts, television often revolves around the theme of justice. Even when we know the story is fictional, something within us roots for justice to be done. We hate the bad guys, cheer for the good guys, and complain if the ending doesn't seem right and good and fair.

Why? Because we care about justice. We're hardwired that way.

The word *justice* can produce two very different feelings depending on context. If you are seeking justice or fighting for justice, then the word is positive. It refers to the idea that you'll finally get what you deserve. Maybe a right that was taken away from you will be restored or you'll get financial recompense for a loss, or someone who committed a crime against you will be charged and convicted. When justice is done, you feel relief, victory, and gratitude.

On the other hand, if someone is running from justice or hiding from justice, the word carries an entirely different meaning. In that case, justice still means the person gets what they deserve—but what that implies for them is punishment and pain.

Let's think about how justice applies to God. God is justice personified. The reason we have an innate sense of justice is because we were created in God's image. It's human to value justice because it's divine to value justice.

But left to our own devices, we get justice terribly wrong, and the breakdown starts with how we see God.

Too often, we live believing that we are on God's bad side. We are, after all, the lawbreakers, the perpetrators, the criminals. As a result, we view God with dread and shame. We don't want to be close to him because it's a reminder of how far short we have fallen. If we receive anything from God, we think, it's going to be punishment and pain.

But that's not the view God has of his children according to Scripture. In Christ, we are on the right side of justice. That means his justice is not a threat that keeps us in line, but a reality that keeps us safe. It's not something he punishes us with, but something he comforts us with. When God calls us righteous, he is calling us his own.

John wrote, "If we claim to be without sin, we deceive ourselves and the truth is not in us. If we confess our sins, he is faithful and just and will forgive us our sins and purify us from all unrighteousness" (1 John 1:8–9).

Notice that phrase "he is faithful and just and will forgive." God's faithfulness and justice are the *reason* he forgives our sins. Because God cannot change, we do not have to wonder if we are forgiven. There are no conditions, no expiration dates, no hidden clauses. Sometimes we are scared of his justice, but actually it's our safeguard and guarantee. Justice must be done, but justice has *already* been established through Jesus.

The problem, of course, is that we keep making mistakes. We continue to sin, to fail, to fall short. That makes it really hard to "feel" righteous. We know ourselves all too well, and we are disappointed in our shortcomings.

We can only imagine how much more disappointed an infinite, perfect, just God must be. If we are mad at ourselves, he must be absolutely furious. If we are out of patience with our weakness, isn't he about to flick us off the planet in disgust?

That is exactly where we need God's tenacious sense of justice. He isn't pursuing us without mercy so we can pay for our sins; he chases us down because we belong to him and to the transforming power of his justice. Jesus ransomed us from sin, offering deliverance from the illusion of self-righteousness. In him, sin doesn't have to be our master. We have been declared righteous.

Obviously that doesn't give us a free pass to sin without consequence. Sin is costly. Period. Intentional, callous sin is a sign of deeper problems—lack of faith in God, of love for him, or of love for others. The fact that you're even reading this book, though, means it's unlikely you are the "callous sinner" type.

But you are human. And humans mess up from time to time. When you do, remember: God is faithful and just, so humble yourself before God and repent of your sins, knowing that you will never stop being forgiven. You will never escape his justice—and that's a good thing.

For further thought, read Romans 8:14 and 1 John 2:12.

REFLECT

1. How does God's justice comfort and safeguard you?

2. Do you tend to see yourself on the right side of God's justice or the wrong side? Why?

3. Is it hard for you to live in the power of forgiveness? Why or why not?

respond

What does it mean to be forgiven? Think of a creative way to illustrate forgiveness in the space below. You might want to draw, write a poem, recount a story from your own life, or simply jot down a few personal thoughts. It's up to you.

GOD IS MERCIFUL,
so i am forgiving

REST

Life has a sneaky way of stacking up layers of stress and anxiety, so before you begin reading, take a couple of minutes to release those layers, one at a time.

Breathe calmly and rhythmically until you are at peace. There's no hurry right now. No urgency. No pressure.

When you are ready, tell yourself, *I am righteous and forever loved. God's mercy is my home, my safe place, my daily reality.*

READ

The Fine Art of Forgiveness   Do you have a friend who is a chronic apologizer? They apologize for everything, whether it's their fault or not. If they are quiet, they are sorry for being so withdrawn. If they talk, they are sorry for being so obnoxious. If they ask questions, they are sorry for being so intrusive. If they talk about themselves, they are sorry for being so self-centered.

When you tell them they don't need to apologize so much, they tell you they are sorry for that too. And when you point out the irony of that cliché, they are sorry for being sorry for being so sorry all the time.

Still, that's preferable to the kind of person who never apologizes for anything, right? Saying sorry too often is a bad habit. Never saying sorry at all is bad character.

We all make mistakes, and most of us learned the value of owning up to those mistakes and moving on a long time ago. That's not fun though. It's humbling. That is exactly why it's so important. Humility is good for the soul, not to mention our relationships.

There's something else we should do nearly as often as we apologize: forgive. Just like saying sorry, granting forgiveness is a necessary part of human existence. Why? Because we tend to let each other down on a regular basis. (Chronic forgivers don't really exist though, and for good reason: if you walked around saying "I forgive you" all the time, you'd come across a bit passive-aggressive.)

In one sense apologizing and forgiving are two sides of the same coin. We have been forgiven, so we forgive. We have received mercy, so we show mercy. The opposite is also true: granting forgiveness and showing mercy make it easier for us to receive forgiveness and mercy. In his letter to the Colossian church, Paul put it this way:

> Therefore, as God's chosen people, holy and dearly loved, clothe yourselves with compassion, kindness, humility, gentleness and patience. Bear with each other and forgive one another if any of you has a grievance against someone. Forgive as the Lord forgave you. (3:12–13)

Giving and receiving forgiveness are based on the same thing: *mercy*. Mercy means not receiving (or not doling out) consequences that are deserved. It's an act of generosity, of compassion, of love.

God's mercy is legendary in the Bible. It's one of his defining characteristics. The prophet Jeremiah wrote, "Because of the LORD's great love we are not consumed, for his compassions never fail. They are new every morning; great is your faithfulness" (Lam. 3:22–23). And Paul said something similar in Ephesians: "Because of his great love for us, God, who is rich in mercy, made us alive with Christ even when we were dead in transgressions—it is by grace you have been saved" (2:4–5). Throughout the Bible, we see that God is passionate about extending mercy to finite, fallible human beings.

As humans, we both give and receive mercy, forgiveness, and grace. But God only gives these things away. He doesn't need to receive them because he never makes mistakes. Despite that, God doesn't hold back when it comes to showing us the mercy we need. Think about it—if anyone could be stingy with their forgiveness, it's God. But he doesn't think or act like that. It's in his nature to be merciful, and he delights in granting us the grace and forgiveness we need.

Because God is so merciful to us, we can be generous with our mercy as well. We can be people who are quick to forgive, even when those we are forgiving are not exactly models of perfection. God sets the example for us by forgiving us when we don't deserve it.

Forgiveness doesn't mean allowing people to continue harming you or others. It doesn't mean pretending that harm never happened or excusing the actions of someone who failed you either. You might need to set boundaries or remove yourself from a situation, and that's okay. But give these dynamics to God. Do not allow unforgiveness to make the hard decisions for you.

Who in your life needs forgiveness? Who needs mercy? And on the flip side, where do *you* need forgiveness and mercy? Make a conscious effort to incorporate mercy into everything you do today.

For further thought, read Matthew 5:43–45; Ephesians 4:32; and Colossians 3:13.

REFLECT

1. Is it easy or difficult to forgive others? Why?

2. What does God's mercy mean to you personally?

3. Are there people around you who need your mercy and forgiveness?

respond

Mercy and forgiveness are beautiful words, but they can be difficult, too, because of what they represent: the existence of hurt, betrayal, and conflict. Use the space provided to express how you view mercy and forgiveness.

GOD IS GRACE,
so i am unstoppable

REST

Before you start today, take time to quiet your mind, emotions, and body. Be intentionally still. Know that God is in control; trust his grace and power.

Let go of the tyranny of the urgent and the voices clamoring for attention in your mind. Listen to the silence, to God's still, small voice that speaks when you quiet the outside noise.

After a couple of minutes, remind yourself, *God's grace surrounds me, holds me, and protects me. I am righteous, so I am unstoppable.*

READ

Getting Back Up Is Spiritual If you study successful businesses or read the memoirs of successful people, you'll notice something: The path to success is rarely easy, quick, or straight. The backstory of what seems to be overnight success often includes years of failed attempts and dogged persistence.

The mistakes and missteps don't get as much airtime as the victories because failure is not a fun topic of conversation. It's painful. Embarrassing. Discouraging. We'd rather ignore or even deny it than talk about it. And yet we all experience failure, probably on a regular basis.

The real question in any endeavor shouldn't be, *How do we avoid all failure?* Instead, we should be asking, *How do we process failure better?*

How do we react to mistakes, tragedy, and loss in a healthy way? How do we get back up when we've fallen down multiple times in a row?

When it comes to following God, the same truth applies. We can't expect the path to always be easy. We will face unexpected events, tragedies, losses, mistakes, and failures. Life is not perfect, and we certainly aren't either.

That's okay. God doesn't ask for perfection, at least not in the way we think of perfection. But he does ask us to get back up and keep moving forward. He'd prefer perseverance over pseudo-perfection any day. When we fall, we must get back up. The writer of Proverbs 24 put it this way: "Though the righteous fall seven times, they rise again, but the wicked stumble when calamity strikes" (v. 16).

Notice the difference between how the "righteous" handle tragedy or loss and how the "wicked" handle it. They both fall, but only the righteous get back up. In Proverbs, the word *righteous* refers to those who are following God and trusting in him. The word *wicked* refers to those who don't acknowledge God or follow his ways. The point of this proverb is that our relationship with God makes us strong, resilient, and unstoppable.

We tend to think that true spirituality and faith mean going from victory to victory. In Jesus, we experience many victories, but getting up after failure, loss, tragedies, or mistakes is actually *more* spiritual than a string of easy victories. Our resilience is proof of our faith and our faithfulness, of our commitment and our confidence.

Our ability to get back up is a direct result of God's grace. If our heavenly Father were an angry, perfectionistic, unforgiving God, then our mistakes would disqualify us. But that's not his attitude at all. Instead, he gives us his grace in our time of need and provides his strength in place of our weakness. As John Bevere tells us, "Grace is God's empowerment to go beyond our natural ability."

The apostle Paul knew how important grace was. Apparently he struggled with an unspecified weakness: Maybe an illness. Maybe an addiction, an enemy, his mental health—we don't really know because he didn't explicitly say.

What we know is that Paul prayed desperately and repeatedly to be set free from it. Here's how he described God's response.

Three times I pleaded with the Lord to take it away from me. But he said to me, "My grace is sufficient for you, for my power is made perfect in weakness." Therefore I will boast all the more gladly about my weaknesses, so that Christ's power may rest on me. (2 Cor. 12:8–9)

We may not know exactly what Paul faced, but we know what *we* face. Fear. Illness. Criticism. Mockery. Delay. Doubt. Slander. Insecurity. Anxiety. Tragedy. Betrayal. Rejection. Shame.

No matter what weakness or failure looks like for you, the same truth that Paul experienced applies. In your weakness, God is strong. In your failures, God is victorious. In your need, God is gracious.

Nothing can keep you from God's grace and love, so nothing can keep you down.

For further thought, read Romans 8:38–39 and Hebrews 4:14–16.

REFLECT

1. What does *grace* mean to you? How does God's grace affect your view of failure?

2. Is it hard to get back up when life knocks you down? Why or why not?

3. In what areas do you need an extra dose of grace today? Are there any goals or projects where you are discouraged and need God to help you keep going?

respond

Use this space to express what failure, grace, and resilience mean to you. How could you describe the pain of failure? How could you illustrate the concepts of strength and courage under pressure? What would a long-awaited victory feel like? As always, use whatever creative medium or expression fits you best.

GOD IS LIGHT,
so i am an advocate

REST

Be silent for a few moments. Imagine God as light, a light that fills you with warmth and peace.

Rest in his light. You have nothing to hide. God doesn't reject the dark parts of your soul; he heals them. He fills you with light. He makes you a light for others.

Breathe out tension, shame, and fear. Breathe in God's love. When you are finished, whisper to yourself, *God sees who I am, and he loves me how I am. I am righteous, safe, and healed.*

READ

Leave the Light On Have you ever washed the dishes or vacuumed the floor in a dimly lit room? When you finished, you were sure all traces of the guacamole you ate for dinner had been washed down the drain and the last stray pet hairs had been removed from the living room.

But the next morning, you realized something: what seemed clean in the evening looked very different in the light of day. A darkened room might be great for a romantic dinner or an evening show, but for deep cleaning the house . . . not so much. For that, you need light. Otherwise, guacamole and pet hair have a way of coming back to haunt you.

In the same way that daylight reveals the spots we overlooked in the darkness, so God's light reveals things in us and in the world around us that we might not have seen before. When we draw close to him, when we open our hearts and lives to him, he begins to spotlight things that need to be addressed.

That's a good thing. Yes, it can be uncomfortable or even frustrating, because we like to think we are cleaner than we really are. But wouldn't you rather God show you the things that are harming you or others, as opposed to allowing your blind spots to continue? He's like the friend you can count on to tell you when you have lettuce in your teeth, your socks don't match, your fly is down, or your breath could use some TLC. You're grateful for that person and for their willingness to tell you what you need to hear, even if it's a little awkward in the moment.

John described God and his light this way:

This is the message we have heard from him and declare to you: God is light; in him there is no darkness at all. If we claim to have fellowship with him and yet walk in the darkness, we lie and do not live out the truth. But if we walk in the light, as he is in the light, we have fellowship with one another, and the blood of Jesus, his Son, purifies us from all sin. (1 John 1:5–7)

Notice the emphasis on *walking* in the light. Walking implies a journey. It speaks of growth and progress. The point of this passage is that as we walk through life—wherever we go, whoever we are with, whatever we face—we are walking with God. We are in his light, and his light illuminates our way.

The result of this is twofold, according to verse 7. First, we have fellowship with one another, and second, we are righteous before God. God's light always connects us to one another and connects us to God.

This is important. God doesn't just highlight the things we've overlooked in our own lives. Often he points out ways we need to help those around us. That could be on an individual level, such as helping an older neighbor with their grocery shopping. Or it could be on a broader level, such as fighting for justice in an area of society.

Light is a metaphor for purity and righteousness, so saying "God is light" means God is pure and righteous. In Jesus, we are also righteous, which means we are also called to be light. Jesus once told his disciples, "While I am in the world, I am the light of the world" (John 9:5). But on another occasion, he passed the torch to them by saying:

> You are the light of the world. A town built on a hill cannot be hidden. Neither do people light a lamp and put it under a bowl. Instead they put it on its stand, and it gives light to everyone in the house. In the same way, let your light shine before others, that they may see your good deeds and glorify your Father in heaven. (Matt. 5:14–16)

God's light reveals where change is needed, and it inspires us to advocate for that change. Because he is light, we are advocates. Because he loves the whole world, we serve the whole world.

This light isn't meant to shame people for their errors any more than God's light shames us. Rather, it's meant to highlight what needs to be fixed for the good of everyone.

Light is a blessing. It's a gift. It brings life, wholeness, and health. When Jesus called us the light of the world, he was calling us to build a world that is defined by love, not hate. A world where people are valued, not ignored. A world that is wide and diverse, not limited to just one group and culture.

Yes, God's light will reveal areas of your life that need attention. But don't limit his light just to you. God will show you needs around you. He will reveal blind spots in systems and structures that you belong to and are called to change. He will ask you to speak up for the oppressed, the forgotten, the silenced.

His light is in you. It's a light the world desperately needs, and it cannot be hidden.

For further thought, read John 1:1–14 and Ephesians 5:8–20.

REFLECT

1. How does the metaphor of God as light affect the way you view him?

2. Has God revealed any blind spots to you lately? How did you respond?

3. What could you do to be a light for the world around you? Are there people you could serve or causes you could join?

respond

In the space below, try to think of a creative, personal way to express the ideas of light and advocacy. What does God's light look like? How does his light show you where the world could be improved, and how do you become that light for a world in need?

GOD IS RIGHTEOUS,
so i am confident

REST

Take two minutes to simply sit still. Be quiet. Be present.

Focus on God's approval of you and his love toward you. You are all that you need to be right now. Let go of insecurity, shame, fear.

Say to yourself, *I am accepted and protected by God, so I am strong and bold.*

READ

Nothing to Hide No one is as smugly confident as the sibling of a child who is being disciplined by their parent. If you have kids of your own, you've seen this for sure. If you don't, maybe you've watched this dynamic play out in nephews and nieces, or perhaps you remember what it felt like in your own childhood.

There is usually a specific look on the face of the innocent child, a mixture of genuine pity and barely concealed satisfaction, like they know they shouldn't be happy their sibling was caught, but at the same time justice is sweet. At least, it is when it happens to the other guy.

While gloating isn't the ideal reaction to justice, *confidence* is a natural result of knowing that you've done nothing wrong. If you are innocent, you know you don't have to live in fear of punishment. Proverbs 28 describes it this way: "The wicked flee though no one pursues, but the righteous are as bold as a lion" (v. 1). Others might be scrambling to cover their tracks or to justify their actions, but you don't need to. You have nothing to fear and nothing to hide.

There are two potential problems with this innocence-equals-confidence connection though. First, we live in a broken world where justice is not always carried out properly. There is no absolute guarantee that our innocence will be upheld. Sometimes we are falsely accused or unjustly treated. This is the exception though. And even when it happens, at least we have a clear conscience before God and ourselves, which should count for a lot.

The second problem is more common: we are rarely innocent. At least, not completely. Maybe we do what's right in one area, but we mess up in two other areas. This is a real problem because, since we are painfully aware of our imperfection, we can never feel completely confident.

This is where our righteousness in Christ makes all the difference. We can't stand confidently and boldly on our own righteousness, but we can stand on *his* righteousness. God's declaration that we are holy, righteous, and innocent in Christ infuses us with true confidence. That is why the writer of Hebrews reminded us to "hold firmly to our confidence and the hope in which we glory" (3:6).

We already know that this righteousness doesn't give us a license to sin freely. The reason sin is sin is because it hurts people, whether the sinner or those around them—and that's why God's love won't tolerate it.

But if we do sin, we don't have to run and hide. We aren't in danger of being kicked out of God's family or rejected by heaven. Our belonging is found and secured in Jesus.

> For we do not have a high priest who is unable to empathize with our weaknesses, but we have one who has been tempted in every way, just as we are—yet he did not sin. Let us then approach God's throne of grace with confidence, so that we may receive mercy and find grace to help us in our time of need. (Heb. 4:15–16)

The "high priest" here is Jesus, of course. The writer of Hebrews was saying that Jesus knows our weaknesses because he walked the same planet we do. He is in heaven right now, listening to our prayers. So when we come before God in our time of need, we are met with mercy and grace, not judgment or rejection.

We want to leave you with this final thought: our boldness to come before God should be reflected in our boldness in life. Spiritual confidence will produce natural confidence, if we let it. This isn't about arrogance or a better-than-thou attitude that religion can too easily breed. Rather, it's the quiet confidence that comes from knowing our past, present, and future are in God's hands, and they are safe there.

For further thought, read Psalm 27:1–2; 112:7; and Acts 4:13; 14:3.

REFLECT

1. Is it difficult to believe that you are righteous in Christ? Why or why not?

2. How would you define *boldness*? What does it look like in your life?

3. What are some ways you could grow in confidence?

respond

What do confidence and boldness look like, feel like, or sound like? Use the space below to express your vision of confidence in whatever way you'd like.

GOD IS COMPASSIONATE,
so i am realistic

REST

Focus on bringing your mind to a place of peace and rest. Let go of the hurry and worry that too easily capture your attention.

Breathe in, breathe out. Feel where you are at and accept that place. Love who God has made you to be. You don't have to be any more than that today.

Tell yourself, *I'm in a good place. Who I am is good, where I am is good, and where I'm going is good.*

READ

Expectation versus Reality   Can you think of an expectation versus reality moment you've had recently?

Maybe you baked a cake you saw on Instagram, and the result was so bad you couldn't even convince your dog it was edible.

Or you attempted to fix a broken water pump in your car with a toolkit you bought at Target and a couple of YouTube videos, and the mechanic's bill to fix your misguided endeavor was three times what the water pump would have cost to fix if you'd taken it to them in the first place.

Or you resurrected some old art supplies and tried to paint a self-portrait, and the result could be the cover art for Hollywood's next horror franchise.

We've all had those moments. Not just in our attempts to learn new skills or create art but also in our attempts to follow God, to navigate life, and to love people. We start off with great intentions and high expectations, only to realize that it is harder than it looks.

God understands. He knows what we are capable of, and he knows what he has called us to do. He is under no illusions that we are going to pull all of this off without messing up a few times. God believes in us, but his belief is realistic, not idealistic. His expectations are based on his knowledge of us and bathed in compassion.

David wrote in Psalm 103:13–14, "As a father has compassion on his children, so the LORD has compassion on those who fear him; for he knows how we are formed, he remembers that we are dust." God knows we are finite and fallible. And he's okay with that. He's proud of who we are and how far we've come. He is cheering us on as we move forward in life, learning and growing and becoming the people he designed us to be.

But in truth, God goes beyond cheering us on from the sidelines. His nature compels him to intermingle with our pain and comfort our souls (2 Cor. 1:3–7). That is true compassion.

We need to receive grace and mercy when we fail, and we need to give other people grace and mercy too. Having faith doesn't mean ignoring human limitations. Rather, it means believing that God can do amazing things in and through those limitations. Faith doesn't deny reality, but it sees beyond it and participates in a greater reality.

If we had to be perfect before God could call and send us, we'd never go anywhere or do anything. We'd be stuck at home, frantically trying to perfect whatever area isn't up to our idealistic expectation yet, up to and including cake baking and car fixing and portrait painting.

God specializes in grace. He is really good at turning brokenness into beauty, at using our weaknesses to accomplish the impossible, at turning our failures into miracles.

His grace and compassion are not a justification for giving up. Quite the opposite. They are motivation to continue, to press on, to grow and improve.

There are few things more discouraging than someone who is always disappointed in you and few things more encouraging than someone who always believes in you. So let this sink in, *God believes in you.* Even when you don't believe in yourself, God doesn't give up on you. Even when your best efforts seem laughable, he sees your potential. We looked at Philippians 1:6 earlier: "He who began a good work in you will carry it on to completion until the day of Christ Jesus." God doesn't give up.

Place your expectations in God's hands. Then enjoy this journey called life, with all its unexpected moments along the way. Be content with where you are but be willing and eager to grow. Celebrate how far you've come while also dreaming about where you want to go. Try your best all day long, then relax in the evening, knowing that who you are and where you are is beautiful to God.

For further thought, read Matthew 9:36; 14:14; and Colossians 3:12.

REFLECT

1. How do you process your frustrations with failures and weaknesses?

2. What does the word *compassion* mean to you? What do you think God's compassion looks like in your life?

3. How would a realistic view of yourself help you process the failures (and successes) you might face in the future?

respond

Take a few minutes to explore the idea of God's compassion for human limitations. What does it mean to you that God knows your weaknesses and doesn't reject you because of them? Can you think of a metaphor or a way to illustrate the relationship you have with this patient, compassionate God?

PART 3
i am loved

I AM LOVED, SO I LOVE WITHOUT RESERVATION. My capacity to give and receive love is beyond measure. I'm protected by the truth that nothing can escape the reach of my Father's love. This eternal love extends beyond the confines of time, connecting every culture, generation, and location. God's perfect love expels all fear, inviting me to love those—including myself—who are "scary" to love. When it's all said and done, I can love others because my Father first loved me. I am loved, so I love without reservation.

GOD IS LOVE,
so i am empathetic

REST

You are loved by God. Set aside any feelings of unworthiness or shame. Set aside your to-do list, your schedule, your phone. Just be loved.

Breathe love in, then breathe it out. Take a couple of minutes to do this. Don't stop until any and all tension evaporates and you find yourself safe in God's arms.

Tell yourself, *I am so loved. I'm deeply, passionately, eternally loved by God himself. And that's enough for me.*

READ

Fully Known, Fully Loved   "If I were you . . ."

You've heard that phrase before. It typically is followed by advice (which you may or may not have asked for) from a friend, a parent, a boss, or an acquaintance. Or worse, some random person online commenting on a vulnerable post of yours. They see something you're facing and decide to tell you what they would do if they were in your place.

You listen or read their words, and while you might be grateful for their good intentions and point of view, you probably also can't help but think, *That's easy for you to say. You aren't the one who has to do that.*

Their advice comes from a good heart, so you give them the benefit of the doubt. But maybe you've been on the receiving end of some really cringeworthy comments about what someone else would supposedly do "if they were you." They don't know what you are *really* going through. They can't see all the details, nuances, and intricacies. They don't see how you feel stuck in a lose-lose scenario, where you are forced to choose the lesser of two evils.

The truth is, they are *not* in your place. If they were, they'd probably make choices similar to yours. And if they didn't, they would soon realize that it's not as simple as it appears from the outside.

To be honest, we all judge too quickly at times. We might criticize our parents—until we become parents ourselves and realize parenting can be messy. Maybe we criticize our boss—until we have employees of our own and discover that decisions are not so black-and-white when you're trying to run a company.

Only when we have lived something from the inside can we understand the complexities of it. And when we do, something happens in our hearts and minds. We treat those who are in similar circumstances differently than before. We begin to show mercy. Compassion. Understanding. Patience.

That doesn't mean we agree with all their choices. That's not the point. The point is to ask ourselves: Can we show each other true empathy? Can we really put ourselves in someone else's place? Will we love people authentically, wading with them into the messiness of life, or will we stand on the outside and offer cheap suggestions?

God could have stood on the outside. Out of anyone, he had the right to shout advice and criticism at us from the comfort of heaven. He didn't have to get his hands dirty. But instead, he came to earth as one of us. In the ultimate act of empathy, God chose to become a human being.

Listen to Paul's description of this in his letter to the Philippians and notice how Jesus intentionally puts himself in our place. Here, Paul was likely quoting an ancient hymn or early Christian poetry.

In your relationships with one another, have the same mindset as Christ Jesus:

> Who, being in very nature God,
> > did not consider equality with God something to be used to his own advantage;

rather, he made himself nothing
    by taking the very nature of a servant,
    being made in human likeness.
And being found in appearance as a man,
    he humbled himself
    by becoming obedient to death—
      even death on a cross! (2:5–8)

Jesus literally came into our world, lived among us, felt what we felt—and ultimately took our place on the cross. From birth to death, he understands what we face as humans.

Now that he has lived among us, do you know what his attitude toward us is? Mercy. Compassion. Understanding. Patience. God always treated us that way, of course, but Jesus's presence among us revealed and confirmed the Father's nature.

He gets us. He knows us. And still, he loves us.

Empathy is part of love. And since God's very nature is love, he continually shows empathy. John wrote, "And so we know and rely on the love God has for us. God is love. Whoever lives in love lives in God, and God in them" (1 John 4:16).

God's empathy toward us should awaken our empathy toward others. We might not be able to physically take their place, but we can get as close as possible. Rather than giving cheap advice or passing quick judgment, we should take the time to be *with* people. To see the world through their eyes. To listen through their ears. To feel with their hearts. To absorb their pain, wrestle with their questions, cry their tears, carry their burdens.

That's what Jesus did. Because that's what love always does.

For further thought, read Matthew 7:1–5 and James 2:12–13.

REFLECT

1. What does *empathy* mean to you? How is it similar to or different than love?

2. How does God show us empathy?

3. Are there specific areas in your life where you'd like to grow in empathy?

respond

What does God's love and empathy toward the world look like? How should that empathy flow through you toward others? Think about how you could express these concepts creatively, using the space below.

GOD IS PATIENT,
so i am enough

REST

Take two minutes before you begin, to center your thoughts and calm your mind. There is no hurry to finish, no rush to get back to the hectic routine of life.

Be present. Relax. Maybe even smile a little. Don't criticize yourself for what you haven't accomplished yet or for the things you still need to change. Enjoy who you are and where you are.

When you are ready, whisper to yourself, *God is enough for me, and I am enough for him.*

READ

You're Not Being Graded   Do you remember the pressure of getting good grades in school? Or maybe not even "good" grades, because good is relative. Maybe just the bare minimum to move to the next grade so that the struggle could start all over again in the fall.

Now, if you are one of the lucky few to whom academics came naturally, that pressure might not have been a big deal. For you, tests, projects, and report cards were not a source of shame or stress, but a badge of honor, a bright spot of self-confidence amid the craziness of school.

The rest of us hate you for that—just kidding. It's not your fault you are God's favorite. Or at least the teacher's favorite.

Honestly, though, did any of us *not* grow up slightly scarred by the pressure of getting the right grades? It's a traumatizing system, if you think about it. Essentially you start out with 100 percent, but every single error reduces that percentage. It's a downhill slope, a constantly increasing debt, a quarter-, semester-, or trimester-long journey further and further from perfection. And the fact that others are getting better grades just drives more nails into your emotional coffin.

Okay, we might be getting a little bit dark here. But still, the system always reminds you that you missed the mark. It's a built-in feature of grading.

Now, whether tests and grades are the best way to teach kids is up to academia and the experts to figure out. But the reality is that many of us, even years after graduating, are still grading ourselves. And we are still coming up short. Why? Because we face life with the same mentality we had in school: Every error is proof that we didn't get it right. That we forgot something. That we made a mistake. That we didn't measure up. That we fell short.

In other words, that we are not enough.

Here's the thing though: *God is not grading you.* Read that again.

God doesn't keep a running list of your failures in a heavenly gradebook. When you lost your temper and took it out on the cat, he didn't give you a demerit. When you gave in to that temptation you swore you'd never fall prey to again, he didn't fail you. When you were addicted or depressed or angry or bitter, he didn't kick you out of class.

God is realistic with all of us. He teaches us, for sure—but his concern is our well-being and our growth, not how we compare to some standardized idea of where we should be by now. God knows how far we've come and how far we have to go, and he's not stressed out by the distance between those points.

That is called patience. Patience is the ability to wait an extended amount of time for an expected result. Patience doesn't lose its cool when things take longer than expected, but it doesn't give up either. It's true realism, not perfectionism or defeatism.

Patience is one of God's defining characteristics. Listen to what Peter wrote about God's patience: "The Lord is not slow in keeping his promise, as some understand slowness. Instead he is patient with you, not wanting anyone to perish, but everyone to come to repentance" (2 Pet. 3:9). A few verses later, he added, "Bear in mind that our Lord's patience means salvation, just as our dear brother Paul also wrote you with the wisdom that God gave him" (v. 15).

Peter was writing about salvation here, but our salvation is only the beginning of a lifetime of transformation and change. God's patience leads to our salvation, and it continues to lead us into all God has for us.

God's patience, not our performance, is why we can have confidence right now. If he were frustrated or impatient with us, then we'd have reason to freak out a little. But assuming we aren't intentionally disobeying God or doing things that clearly hurt people, we should probably take some deep breaths and stop obsessing over our spiritual grade point average (because that's not even a thing) and just focus on following Jesus.

We'll get where we are going—but we don't have to get there today. God is patient, and we are enough right now.

For further thought, read 1 Corinthians 1:4–9; 13:4.

REFLECT

1. How have you seen God's patience at work in your life?

2. Do you ever struggle with thinking you are not enough? Why or why not?

3. How does God's patience enable you to be more patient with yourself? With others?

respond

Can you express the concepts of patience and "being enough" using words, poetry, a picture, or some other creative means? Take a few minutes to illustrate what these ideas signify to you, using the space below.

GOD IS SKILLFUL,
so i am valuable

REST

Breathe slowly for two minutes before you move on. This is a time to release anything that is distracting you from God. If you feel insufficient, trust God's sufficiency. If you feel anxious or worried, cast your cares on God. If you feel ashamed, let God's grace replace the condemnation.

Let it all go: worry, fear, self-doubt, shame, stress. Give it to God. He can carry it better than you.

When you're ready, tell yourself, *God made me, and he has chosen me. I am worthy. I am loved. I am valuable.*

READ

Just Tell Me What It's Worth   Have you ever watched those shows where experts appraise random items—antiques, jewelry, pieces of art—and reveal their true value?

The item often looks worthless, dirty, ugly, neglected. The episode usually starts by digging into the backstory of the item and its owner. Maybe the object was discovered in the attic of a relative who recently passed on or it has been handed down from generation to generation, or it was purchased at a garage sale fifteen years ago. The expert examines the item, discusses it a bit, and finally gets to the part everyone really cares about—its monetary value.

When that number is finally announced, the camera always pans to the owner's face. If the value is lower than expected, their disappointment is clear. But when the value is higher—like, ridiculously higher—their reaction of stunned joy is contagious. You find yourself smiling along with them. Then, of course, your mind jumps to all the old things your family has stashed away, and you start dreaming about finding something valuable that is gathering dust in *your* grandma's attic.

Value is a funny thing. It is determined not by some objective rulebook, but by *demand*. In other words, by who wants it and how badly. That's why some of the most valuable things you might find in basements and attics are old baseball cards, unopened video games, and vintage toys. They are worth far more now than when they were first sold. Why? Because they are rare, and because they are in high demand.

Rare artwork is incredibly valuable. When a painting by a master artist is stolen, or when a lost masterpiece is rediscovered, it makes headlines around the world. Not only is the piece one of a kind, but the creator is famous for their skill as an artist. Some pieces of art are worth millions of dollars.

Now think for a moment about God as Creator. He is not in the business of mass-producing humans, despite the fact that there are over eight bil-lion of us. Instead, God is a skillful, expert artisan, the greatest master of all, who creates one-of-a-kind works of art. And we are in demand by *him*. We are both extremely rare and highly wanted, which translates to great value.

Read these words from David, and listen to how he connected God's creative skill with his own sense of self-worth:

> For you created my inmost being;
>   you knit me together in my mother's womb.
> I praise you because I am fearfully and wonderfully made;
>   your works are wonderful,
>   I know that full well.
> My frame was not hidden from you
>   when I was made in the secret place,
>   when I was woven together in the depths of the earth.

Your eyes saw my unformed body;
    all the days ordained for me were written in your book
    before one of them came to be.
How precious to me are your thoughts, God!
    How vast is the sum of them!
Were I to count them,
    they would outnumber the grains of sand—
    when I awake, I am still with you. (Ps. 139:13–18)

Notice how David emphasized both his uniqueness and his importance to God. He was "fearfully and wonderfully made" and his days were "ordained" and written in God's book. In other words, God—the skillful master creator—intentionally formed David to fulfill a specific destiny, and that gave him immense value.

You might not *feel* valuable at times, particularly if you've let your value be determined by what other people say about you or by how much money you're making or by your follower count on Instagram. But if you turn to God, if you put your life before him and ask him what you're worth, it will be your turn to stand there in stunned joy as you realize just how valuable you are.

So sure, go ahead and dig through those dusty boxes at your grandma's house, looking for forgotten treasures. But don't forget to look at yourself while you're at it. That's where the real treasure is.

For further thought, read John 15:16 and 2 Thessalonians 2:13–14.

REFLECT

1. Do you feel valuable? Why or why not?

2. How can you see God's skill at work in you? What gifts or talents has he given you?

3. How could your uniqueness be of service to others?

respond

Think for a moment about how valuable you are to God and to the world around you, then write or draw something that illustrates your value.

GOD IS GIVING,
so i am content

REST

Take a moment to gauge what you are feeling. Notice what is filling your mind or affecting your heart.

Breathe in, breathe out. Let the pressures and stress melt away and allow God's peace and joy to begin to grow.

After a couple of minutes, remind yourself, *God is good, life is good, and I am good. I am fulfilled and content.*

READ

I'm Good, Thanks   Want to make some questionable financial choices? Go grocery shopping when you're hungry. The mistakes will start adding up (and so will your tab).

When you're starving, everything looks delicious—so you throw every-thing in the cart. Sometimes two or three of everything, just in case. When you get to the checkout, the bill is more than your rent. When you stuff it all into the car, the trunk will hardly close. When you get home, the refrigerator groans audibly when it sees you.

The only thing worse than shopping while hungry is shopping with *kids* who are hungry. They want everything they see, and they don't have the emotional intelligence to refrain from yelling when their cravings are denied.

When you're hungry, your brain automatically tells your body to start hunting for food. It's a survival instinct that works great when you are at home, because all you have to do is stroll into the kitchen and browse through the refrigerator. But that instinct backfires dramatically when you're shopping for the week and you throw a month's worth of cereal and fruit into the cart.

That same survival instinct tends to kick in when we have lack in *any* area. When there is a need, we might find ourselves suddenly and urgently wanting to meet it however we can. That feeling can be overpowering, and it can lead us to desperation and excess. Maybe it's job security, maybe it's a health challenge, maybe it's loneliness, maybe it's financial hardship—whatever the need is, the tendency will be to fixate on that need until it's met.

Here's the thing though: Like hungry children in grocery stores, sometimes we need to grow in our emotional intelligence. Just because we have a need right now doesn't mean the need has to be *met* right now. And it definitely doesn't mean we should throw everything in the store (or everything in our imaginations or desires) into meeting that need. It's healthy to take a step back from the issues that are captivating our attention and make sure we are approaching them with a mature, patient attitude, not an urgent, "give it to me now or I might scream" attitude.

One way to describe this patient attitude is being *content*. Contentment means you don't need anything else to be happy. To be content is to be satisfied. To be fulfilled. To be at peace emotionally, even when things are less than ideal. It's when you can look at yourself and honestly say, "I'm good now, thanks. I'm taken care of. I'm happy. I'm at peace."

Paul described it this way:

> I have learned to be content whatever the circumstances. I know what it is to be in need, and I know what it is to have plenty. I have learned the secret of being content in any and every situation, whether well fed or hungry, whether living in plenty or in want. I can do all this through him who gives me strength. (Phil. 4:11–13)

Contentment doesn't mean everything is okay—it means that *you* are okay. You can long for change and still be content. You can dream big and still be content. You can work hard and still be content. The difference is that you do these things from a place of inner peace, satisfaction, and happiness.

The best way to be truly content—maybe the only way—is to know that God is taking care of you. When you keep in mind that God is always generous, always present, and always providing, you short-circuit the instinct to panic-buy everything in sight. You realize you don't need to overreact to your needs because God isn't going anywhere. He's there for you. He will continue to meet your needs, big and small, day in and day out, forever. That means you can relax now, even if you have needs that are not yet met. Like Paul, you can be content regardless of your circumstances.

God is a giving, generous, attentive God. There is no safer place to be than in his arms of love.

Also, making a shopping list in advance is helpful. Just throwing that out there.

For further thought, read Psalm 145:13–21 and Hebrews 13:5–6.

REFLECT

1. How would you describe *contentment*? How is being content different from giving up?

2. Are there areas of your life where you find it difficult to be content? Why?

3. How could God's generosity help you remain content even in times of need?

respond

What does God's generosity mean for you? What does contentment feel like or look like? Use the space provided to illustrate these concepts in whatever creative way fits you best.

GOD IS RELATIONAL,
so i am inclusive

REST

Settle your mind and heart for a few minutes before continuing. If it's helpful, use breathing techniques or any other method you prefer to slow down.

Let God's peace consume you. Take on his love, his joy, his righteousness. If you are anxious or stressed, give those things to him. Find rest for your soul.

When you're ready to continue, breathe out, *I am included in God's love. I am welcome in his presence. I am inclusive in my love for others.*

READ

Who's the New Kid?   When was the last time you were "the new kid on the block"? Not just literally, but in any scenario. Maybe you started a new job or you moved to a new place or you began attending a new church. What emotions did you experience in those first days, weeks, and months as you built new relationships? You likely felt a bit vulnerable, nervous, shy, excited, insecure, confident—or all of the above.

We've all been there. Regardless of your personality, stepping into an environment where everybody else has preestablished relationships can be challenging. You are the new kid, the odd person out. It's a little awkward until you start to find your place. Eventually, people make room for you, new friendships form (and maybe a romance too), bonds are built, memories are made, and you start to feel at home.

God created humans with a need to belong. We are hardwired to build social connections, and those connections are important in many ways. They give us safety, motivation, acceptance, information, stability, and more.

Our need for connection is a direct reflection of God's relational nature. From the very beginning we see God interacting with humanity in the garden of Eden. Throughout the Bible God continually speaks to people, works with people, changes people, and loves people. The greatest demonstration of God's love for us, of course, is Jesus coming to earth. Could there be any clearer way to show that God wants to be with us? John wrote this about Jesus: "The Word became flesh and made his dwelling among us" (1:14).

God doesn't just want us to have a relationship with him though. He wants us to have relationships with one another. Going back to Genesis, God created *two* people—Adam and Eve—because he said it was "not good for the man to be alone" (2:18). David wrote about God's heart for relationship as well: "A father to the fatherless, a defender of widows, is God in his holy dwelling. God sets the lonely in families" (Ps. 68:5–6).

God builds communities of people. That's his nature, and it informs our need. Belonging to friend groups, church groups, work groups, or any other group is part of our nature.

Think back to how awkward it felt to try to fit into a preexisting group. You might be comfortable now, but consider others around you who are still alone. Still lonely. Still searching for human connection. Part of your calling as a child of God is to be inclusive of others.

Inclusivity means keeping your heart and your mind open to people who are different from you. It doesn't mean you have to approve of everything they do or love everything about them. You don't have to be their best friend or give them full access to your life from day one. But you do have to love them. No, you *get* to love them. They will bring richness and expansion to your life that you need, and you will do the same for them.

It's easy to remain in your comfort zone of family, friends, and companions, but easy is overrated. Easy leads to a smaller world, not a larger one. To a self-focused existence, not an others-focused one.

Never close your heart to new people. Instead, be the first one to welcome them. You never know, they might become your new best friend or a potential business partner or even a romantic interest. You can't see the future, but you can see the person in front of you. And that person needs to be welcomed and included.

For further thought, read John 13:34–35.

REFLECT

1. Do you find it easy or difficult to meet people and make friends?

2. What makes you feel welcomed by others? How can you make others feel welcomed?

3. Do you consider yourself open and inclusive in your relationships? Do your current friendships reflect that value?

respond

What does inclusivity mean to you? Use the space below to write or draw something that illustrates God's expansive, wide-open heart. Alternately, think about how God "sets the lonely in families" and what that looks and feels like for you.

GOD IS GLOBAL,
so i am an ally

REST

Get comfortable and focus on relaxing for a little while. It's a lot easier to contemplate God if your mind isn't full of distractions.

Breathe calmly. Let the hurry and rush of the day fade. This is a safe place, a peaceful place, a restful place.

When you are ready, whisper, *God sees me, hears me, and loves me, so I can see, hear, and love others too.*

READ

You've Got a Friend in Me   Have you ever cared deeply about something but felt alone in your passion?

It might be something relatively minor, like being the only person who roots for a particular football team or the only one who cares about the quality of the coffee in the employee lounge.

Or it could be something far more significant, such as fighting against an injustice that nobody seems to care about.

Hopefully at some point, you found an ally in your cause. Maybe it was the most unlikely person of all, someone with a different background, different personality, different friend group—but when you discovered what you had in common, the differences didn't matter. What mattered was that you were better together.

Remember *Toy Story*, the Disney classic about a boy and his toy cowboy, Woody? The movie shows a montage of the two playing together while the theme song repeats, "You've got a friend in me." Then trouble in the form of a shiny space ranger named Buzz Lightyear shows up, and the rest of the movie is an all-too-relatable struggle with insecurity and competition—until Woody and Buzz move past their differences and become allies.

"You've got a friend in me" is a great way to describe an ally, actually. More precisely defined, an *ally* is "someone who joins with another in a mutually beneficial relationship."

In Ecclesiastes 4:9–12, Solomon wrote,

> Two are better than one,
>   because they have a good return for their labor:
> If either of them falls down,
>   one can help the other up.
> But pity anyone who falls
>   and has no one to help them up.
> Also, if two lie down together, they will keep warm.
>   But how can one keep warm alone?
> Though one may be overpowered,
>   two can defend themselves.
> A cord of three strands is not quickly broken.

Solomon was right. Two are better than one, and three are better still. Allies give us strength, protection, and aid when we need them the most.

Why do we need to be allies, and why do we need allies? Because we are not self-sufficient, and the world is a long way from being the paradise of peace and love that God originally designed. There are countless people who need to hear the good news that God is their ally and see that truth animated in the lives of others.

We can't be saviors—only God can save. But together we can reflect God's love wherever we go, and we can work for change in the world around us. That's our calling and our responsibility.

One of the best parts of the definition of allyship is that this is a mutually beneficial arrangement. In other words, we aren't swooping in to save the day out of pity. We aren't superior to those we are serving or those we are serving alongside. Rather, we are working together to build a future that is better for all of us. That might mean working for equality or speaking up for victims of violence or countless other causes.

Keep in mind that to be an ally means you stand *with* someone and *for* someone. But it doesn't automatically mean you stand *against* someone else. That's the part that often gets overlooked. We tend to organize into factions and turn justice into vengeance. That is never helpful. Other people are not the enemy—the real enemy is the dark cosmic powers that oppress our humanity (see Eph. 6:12). When we vilify others, we perpetuate the victim/villain dynamic. What's behind the violence and hatred largely goes unaddressed so it just takes on new forms in new generations.

So, where do we go from here? How do we fight to win God's way?

The famous story of the good Samaritan in Luke 10 is a perfect starting point. It's a story about an unlikely ally loving his neighbor—but Jesus's definition of *neighbor* was a lot broader than people expected. Your neighbor is any person in need around you. Your neighbor is the one God has called you to love and care for. Your neighbor is the one who needs an ally, and you are called to be that ally. So, start there.

For further thought, read Luke 10:25–37 and John 3:16–17.

REFLECT

1. What does being an ally mean to you?

2. What causes or areas of injustice are you most passionate about addressing? How can you get involved?

3. In what specific ways could you be an ally to those around you?

respond

Consider for a moment God's love for the whole world, then reflect on *your* role in it. You might imagine the darkness and injustice you are aware of now, or you might envision a better future. If you can think of a creative way to illustrate your thoughts on the subject, use the space below to do so.

PART 4
i am secure

I AM SECURE, SO I LIVE FROM A PLACE OF PEACE. A life of peace is my inheritance. It's part of my family legacy. I live knowing that peace isn't found in having all the answers—it comes from being in tune with the One who has all the answers. In my Father, I am secure. His Spirit wraps me in eternal promises. He orders my steps and fills my life with unexpected brilliance. There's joy in knowing that my future is greater than what I can see in this moment. My life is bigger than what I can build with my hands. I am secure, so I live from a place of peace.

GOD IS FAITHFUL,
so i am peaceful

REST

Relax for a few minutes. Let any tension or worry fall away as you lean into God. This is a time to simply be here, to be yourself, without any expectations or demands.

Close your eyes and breathe slowly, intentionally.

When you are ready, repeat to yourself, *I am secure in God. I am safe in his faithfulness, and I am at peace.*

READ

Sleep like a Baby   The difference between a screaming baby and a sleeping baby is obvious to everyone.

If you've ever babysat an infant, or if you have kids of your own, you know this. One minute, the child is red-faced, sputtering, angry at everything and everybody. The next, they are sleeping angelically, with the most relaxed expression imaginable on their face. The transformation is unbelievable.

The look on an infant's face when they are asleep is the definition of peace. Calm. Serene. Without a care in the world. Absolutely unconcerned about the future. It's where the phrase "sleep like a baby" comes from.

As kids grow up they learn about responsibility, planning, and work. They realize they can't just shut their eyes and expect someone else to meet their needs. As they mature into adults, they scream less and worry more. They grow in emotional intelligence, but they develop a tendency toward anxiety, stress, and fear.

That's where many of us are at, isn't it? We can't fully relax. We can't totally trust. There's always a pinprick of fear in the back of our minds, reminding us that if we don't watch out for ourselves, nobody will.

We do need to watch out for ourselves, of course. Personal responsibility is important. But that doesn't mean we are solely responsible for our lives, or that if we lower our guard everything will fall apart. Regardless of how young or old we are, God is still watching over us.

The author of Psalm 121 said, "He will not let your foot slip—he who watches over you will not slumber; indeed, he who watches over Israel will neither slumber nor sleep" (vv. 3–4). When night falls, we can sleep like a baby because our God never sleeps. He is always faithful to care for us.

God's faithfulness brings us peace. That means he doesn't let us down. He doesn't go back on his word, change his mind, or forget his promises.

It doesn't mean life is easy. We still have to plan ahead and work hard. We will face things we don't understand and go through pain we wish we could avoid. But through it all, God remains faithful. As he reminds us in the book of Hebrews, "Never will I leave you; never will I forsake you" (13:5).

Jesus told his disciples,

> But the Advocate, the Holy Spirit, whom the Father will send in my name, will teach you all things and will remind you of everything I have said to you. Peace I leave with you; my peace I give you. I do not give to you as the world gives. Do not let your hearts be troubled and do not be afraid. (John 14:26–27)

In other words, the Spirit is with us, and Jesus's peace is too. The two are connected. The peace of God doesn't come from having a problem-free life, but from the presence of a faithful God. His peace comes through his presence.

What areas of your life need this kind of peace? Think about the things that feel out of control or beyond your ability, the things that seem like too much for you. Think about the secret fears or nagging doubts that might creep into your mind at night. Then consider God's faithfulness. Let his constant presence and his unbreakable promises bring you peace.

You might feel like screaming like a baby from time to time. We all do. Try to avoid that though. It tends to scare people within earshot. Instead, trust that you are safe in God's arms and always under his gaze. When you believe that, you really can begin to sleep like a baby.

For further thought, read Psalm 131:1–3 and Philippians 4:4–7.

REFLECT

1. What does *peace* mean to you? What would a peaceful life look and feel like?

2. Are there areas where it is difficult for you to trust God and find peace?

3. What are some practical strategies to worry less and trust God more?

respond

Think about what peace looks like for you and how God's faithfulness creates it. Then, using the space below, write or draw something that illustrates your vision of a peaceful life.

GOD IS ACCEPTING,
so i am honest

REST

For two full minutes, be as still and quiet as you can. Don't just calm your body but also calm your mind and your emotions.

Find security in God's acceptance of you. Be fully you and give all of yourself to him.

When you feel ready, whisper, *I am accepted and approved by God. I am good. I am enough.*

READ

Healthy TMI   Do you have a friend who is a chronic oversharer? Or are *you* that friend?

Oversharers tend to say too much, too quickly, too often. Like sharing the gory details of their recent surgery on a first date. Or describing a fight they just had with their friend to a random stranger on the bus. Or revealing embarrassing details about a significant other to a circle of mutual friends who will never, ever let them forget it. The life of a habitual oversharer is an open book—the good, the bad, and the ugly on display for everyone to see. For this person there is no such thing as "too much information."

Sometimes these TMI conversations lead to awkward moments. But this level of confidence is also a little refreshing. For most of us oversharing is probably the exception, and we trend toward the opposite: undersharing. Rather than *divulging* the embarrassing parts of our lives with everyone, we *hide* them. We put on a facade of perfection, a false front designed to convince people we are wonderful, awesome, and capable in every way.

Why? There could be many reasons, but the most obvious is fear of rejection. We think that if people see who we really are, they'll think less of us. They'll mock us. They'll leave us. So we do whatever it takes to keep the embarrassing stuff hidden, lest we lose the friends or the job or the reputation we've worked so hard to achieve.

We might be able to fool the people around us for a while, but eventually they'll see us for who we really are. Most of the time, the rejection we feared never happens. Those close to us love us for who we really are, with all our quirks and idiosyncrasies. If they don't, they aren't the kind of friends we need, anyway.

If the people who care for us can look past our faults, don't you think God can too? God is the *best* at accepting us for who we really are. He already knows all our weaknesses, after all. There is nothing hidden from him. He knows us better than anyone, and he loves us more than everyone.

Paul, the man who penned a good chunk of the New Testament, was honest about his weaknesses, failures, and needs. He wrote:

> Here is a trustworthy saying that deserves full acceptance: Christ Jesus came into the world to save sinners—of whom I am the worst. But for that very reason I was shown mercy so that in me, the worst of sinners, Christ Jesus might display his immense patience as an example for those who would believe in him and receive eternal life. (1 Tim. 1:15–16)

In this passage, he referenced his behavior before knowing Jesus without sugarcoating it. He saw his past self as "the worst of sinners." In other letters, Paul was just as honest about his current struggles: about sin and temptation (see Rom. 7), personal weakness (see 2 Cor. 12:9–10), betrayal and opposition (see 2 Tim. 4:9–18), fear (see 1 Cor. 2:3), and hardship (see 2 Cor. 11:23–33).

Paul was honest. Some would say maybe too honest at times. He wasn't afraid to state his needs, fears, and frustrations because he didn't live in fear of being rejected by God. He knew he could be honest with himself, with his heavenly Father, and with those around him. In a world obsessed with maintaining appearances at all costs, this kind of confident honesty is a breath of fresh air.

Like Paul, we can be confident in God's acceptance of us. If God loved us and called us when we were "the worst of sinners," he isn't going to give up on us now. Rather than pretending we are perfect, we can be honest with our needs, our weaknesses, our failures, and our fears. And when we are honest, we find the grace to grow.

How about you? Are you honest with yourself? With God? With others? Or do you struggle to open your heart and let the real you be seen?

Learn to lean into God's unconditional acceptance of you. Let his love assure you that you are in a safe place. Be honest. Admit what you need, where you've failed, why you're afraid.

Confidence in God's acceptance will help you be more honest with people around you too. Yes, there are still topics you should probably avoid discussing on first dates. Don't hide your true self though. Don't put up a facade because you're afraid to be real.

God loves the real you. Other people—at least, the right people—will too. *For further thought, read Romans 5:6–10 and Ephesians 1:3–14.*

REFLECT

1. Are you more of an oversharer or an undersharer? Why?

2. Do you ever struggle with fear of rejection? If so, how does that affect you? How do you deal with it?

3. How could you be more self-aware and open about the areas you need to grow in?

respond

What does God's acceptance feel like to you? How does his acceptance create a safe place for you to be honestly and authentically *you*? In the space below use words, poetry, lyrics, or a picture to illustrate your thoughts.

DAY 21

GOD IS ALL-SEEING,
so i am open

REST

As you get started today, take two minutes just to be still. Let the hurry and rush of life fade into the background as your soul comes alive.

Breathe in, breathe out, breathe in again. Focus on exchanging stress for rest, shame for acceptance, fear for faith.

When you are finished, whisper to yourself, *I am secure in God. I am confident in myself. I am open to God, open to love, and open to others.*

READ

Check Your Blind Spot   Have you ever started to change lanes on a highway only to realize—usually because you hear panicked and/or angry honking—that there is a car cruising along beside you, just out of sight, and you almost ran them off the road?

Maybe you had checked your rearview mirror, glanced out the window, and were sure you were alone. But you forgot to check your blind spot, that irritating little area near your back bumper where an entire car can hide unnoticed. It's a scary feeling, not to mention an embarrassing one.

If you've been there, hopefully honking and a minor heart attack were all you suffered. The worst that could happen, of course, is causing harm to someone else or to you. Damage to your car can be fixed, and damage to your pride might not be a bad thing. But when blind spots cause real harm, when they hurt you or others, that's serious.

Blind spots are not limited to driving, unfortunately. We can have blind spots in just about any area: our character, our relationships, our logic, our emotions, our finances. Humans, like cars, have blind spots. And humans, like the drivers of those cars, need to pay attention to their blind spots before they run somebody off the road.

The obvious problem with blind spots is that we don't see them. That's the definition of the term, after all. They are places where we are unaware of what is really happening. We assume things are fine. We might be absolutely certain they are. But they aren't. And sometimes, everyone but us can see that.

It takes effort (and a good dose of humility) to find and address those places of ignorance before they cause harm. Again, that's totally normal. Growing and learning are moments to celebrate, not to be embarrassed about. The only embarrassing thing would be to insist that we have no blind spots at all—no areas where we are wrong or deceived or ignorant—and continually veer into harm's way.

We looked yesterday at the importance of being honest. However, honesty starts by recognizing that we might not know what we need to change. We need God's help to see the parts of our lives that still need some work.

God sees everything. That's one of the perks of being omniscient. He doesn't have blind spots of his own, but he can see everybody else's. If he were an angry, impatient, perfectionistic God, that would be terrifying. But he's not. He is love, he is mercy, and he is *truth*. All at the same time.

That means we can go to him to get help in finding out where we are broken. He already sees and knows everything about us, and he loves us madly anyway. There is no need to fear him or dread what he might say. Instead, we can receive his instruction and correction humbly, knowing that his truth and grace set us free.

In Psalm 139:23–24, David wrote, "Search me, God, and know my heart; test me and know my anxious thoughts. See if there is any offensive way in me, and lead me in the way everlasting." He was willing to open his heart to

God because he trusted him. David knew that it was to his benefit to allow God to point out the areas that needed to change.

It takes courage and humility to be as honest and self-aware as David. It's not easy to confront your faults or open yourself up to critique. God loves you unconditionally, so you are safe with him. He's not going to reject you just because you made a mistake or because you still struggle with a weakness.

Yes, there are areas where you need to grow, blind spots the Father will bring to your attention. Remember though, his transformation is more for you than for him. Your weaknesses are not his focus or his obsession. *You* are his focus, his obsession. Changes will come. Growth will happen. Just keep opening yourself up to his good work.

For further thought, read Psalm 51 and Jeremiah 17:9–10.

REFLECT

1. Is it difficult to recognize when you are wrong? Why or why not?

2. When you are told by someone that you have a problem or have made a mistake, how do you tend to respond? Is that a healthy or unhealthy response?

3. What areas of your life might need examination or change?

respond

Use this space to express what the concept of being open and willing to change means to you. You might jot down your thoughts about God's knowledge of everything, draw something that illustrates your growth journey, or write a poem about who you are becoming.

GOD IS ALL-POWERFUL,
so i am safe

REST

Take a moment to focus on God. There is no rush, no hurry, no better place to be right now.

Listen to your body. Listen to your emotions. How are you feeling? You don't need to fix anything in this moment. Just give it to God.

Then say to yourself, *I am here in God's arms where I am safe and secure.*

READ

Safe at Last   Have you ever noticed how highly individualized fear is? That is, we all fear different things, and we fear them at varying levels. It seems a bit random. Some people can ride roller coasters all day long, but they run at the sight of spiders. Others have no problem speaking in front of thousands of people, but they are terrified of the dark. Some are fascinated by bugs, but they get creeped out by clowns.

Not only do we have different fears, but we also experience those fears differently. Fears affect us in unique ways, and our response might be the opposite of someone else's. We might run away or we might fight. We might ask for help or take matters into our own hands. We might feel intense emotion or turn stone-cold.

Our reaction to spiders or clowns is relatively easy to deal with. Just avoid them. Or close your eyes. Or leave the room. But there are a lot of other things that can awaken fear in us that are not so easy to deal with. Fear of death, for example. Or of loss, rejection, pain, financial ruin, health issues, family problems, and much more.

Regardless of what we fear or how we react to it, we can all agree on this: living in fear is not a good thing. It negatively affects our lives. It limits us, it skews our reactions, and it steals our joy.

Here's the good news: God is all-powerful. He is sovereign over everything and everybody. There is no fear or threat or risk that is outside of his domain.

In the Bible the nations around Israel worshiped many gods. These gods were small, limited gods who, according to pagan beliefs, ruled over just one or two things. They were gods of war, for example, or fertility or rain or death. Not only did people have to worry about their day-to-day lives, but they also had to figure out how to appease or manipulate all these mini gods. It was a mess.

Not Israel though. God revealed himself to Abraham, Isaac, and Jacob, and later on to Moses and all of Israel, as the one true God. The only God. The God of everything. And most importantly, the God who cares about humanity.

What does God's sovereignty have to do with fear? It means that no matter what makes us anxious and worried, we are safe because God is in control. We don't have to go from source to source trying to find security. God isn't bigger than just one threat; he's bigger than all the threats. He doesn't just have answers to some questions; he has answers to all the questions. He doesn't just have power over one thing; he has power over everything.

The book of Psalms has countless reminders of the safety we find in God. One of the most famous is Psalm 91.

> If you say, "The Lord is my refuge,"
>   and you make the Most High your dwelling,
> no harm will overtake you,
>   no disaster will come near your tent.

For he will command his angels concerning you
to guard you in all your ways;
they will lift you up in their hands,
so that you will not strike your foot against a stone. (vv. 9–12)

God's sovereignty is our safety. No matter what makes us anxious or causes us to feel unsafe, it will never fall outside of God's knowledge or power.

That doesn't mean we will never have problems or pain. Life has a lot of difficult moments, and sometimes what we fear, or part of it, does come to pass. But it does mean that problems and pain cannot destroy us. Rather than living in fear, we can trust that anything that happens will be within the realm of God's sovereignty. Including but not limited to thwarting spiders, darkness, and clowns.

God can keep us safe in even the most difficult circumstances. Not only that but in his sovereignty, he brings good out of evil. When we look back over our lives, we often see that what we feared would destroy us actually made us stronger, better, and more complete.

True safety is not the absence of loss or fear or pain, but the assurance that God is sovereign over it all. We are not alone. We are safe in the arms of an all-powerful, always-loving God.

For further thought, read Psalm 91 and 1 John 5:18.

REFLECT

1. Would you say that you generally feel safe? Why or why not?

2. Are there fears that you have a difficult time overcoming?

3. How could the knowledge of God's power and goodness help you address fear?

respond

Think about God's sovereignty and imagine being completely safe in his arms. What does safety feel like or look like to you? Use the space provided to describe or illustrate this in whatever creative way feels best to you.

GOD IS ALL-KNOWING,
so i am provided for

REST

Take a couple of minutes to be fully present and fully you. Take up the space that belongs to you, the space God created you to fill. You are here and that matters.

Let go of expectations, of control, of perfectionism, of guilt.

Finish by whispering, *I am seen, I am safe, and I am secure. My needs are met, and my future is good.*

READ

God Never Guesses   Have you ever hit Send on a text only to realize a split second too late that autocorrect decided to "fix" something you typed? Maybe the result was worse than embarrassing—it was borderline obscene. If the text was to a close friend or significant other, it's good for a few laughs. But if it was to a business contact, a client, or your boss . . . that's another story.

The problem with autocorrect is that it doesn't know what you meant to say. It has great intentions (well, the makers of the technology do), but the autocorrect feature has no way of peering inside your brain. So as you type, it runs its magical, mysterious algorithms and takes a semi-educated guess at what you probably meant to say. Sometimes it nails it. Other times, not so much.

Humans have made incredible progress with technology in the last few decades, but it's unlikely a phone will ever be able to read our minds. That means we'll be dealing with autocorrect fails for a long time to come. God, on the other hand, *can* see inside our minds. He knows what we think, dream, fear, want, hope for, and plan to do next. God does not rely on algorithms. He's not artificial intelligence. He's not a chatbot or predictive text or a phone tree or any of the other strategies humans have invented to try to solve people's problems automatically.

God is our Father. He is personally involved with us, and he sees everything and knows everything about our situation. He knows where we came from, where we are, and where we are going. He is aware of what we need before we do, and he already has a plan to supply it. Because God knows everything, we can trust him to care for us. Listen to Jesus's words to his disciples:

> Therefore I tell you, do not worry about your life, what you will eat or drink; or about your body, what you will wear. Is not life more than food, and the body more than clothes? Look at the birds of the air; they do not sow or reap or store away in barns, and yet your heavenly Father feeds them. Are you not much more valuable than they? Can any one of you by worrying add a single hour to your life? . . .
>
> So do not worry, saying, "What shall we eat?" or "What shall we drink?" or "What shall we wear?" For the pagans run after all these things, and your heavenly Father knows that you need them. But seek first his kingdom and his righteousness, and all these things will be given to you as well. (Matt. 6:25–27, 31–33)

Jesus couldn't have made it clearer: God cares about us, he knows what we need, and he is taking care of us. Worry and anxiety, therefore, are not helpful. Living in fear is unnecessary.

God's care for us usually includes our participation. We know that. We've been given resources to manage, talents to use, opportunities to explore, and the strength and creativity we need to problem-solve.

It's also important to remember that God's care for us doesn't always manifest the way we think it should, at least not in the moment. *Life shouldn't be this difficult*, we sometimes think. *Either I'm doing something wrong or God's not paying attention.*

Those are the moments we most need to trust him. All we can see is what we're experiencing now, but God sees the next chapter—and every chapter—of our entire story. He knows how he's going to take care of us today, and he also knows how best to lead us into the future. Even when the path doesn't make sense, God is with us. As David famously wrote, "Even though I walk through the darkest valley, I will fear no evil, for you are with me; your rod and your staff, they comfort me" (Ps. 23:4).

God knows what you need. The waiting season doesn't mean he is ignoring you or indifferent toward you. It doesn't mean you messed up somewhere and ruined it all. Trust the God who knows your needs better than anyone, including you. Stay faithful, stay full of faith, and keep walking. The valley will end, the darkness will fade into memory, and your needs will be met.

For further thought, read Isaiah 43:1–2 and Philippians 4:18.

REFLECT

1. Are there any areas where you urgently need God's provision?

2. Do you tend to worry over anything? If so, what things worry you most, and why?

3. How does the fact that God knows everything affect your perspective on life?

respond

How could you describe or illustrate the truth that God knows about and cares for your needs? Is there a symbol, picture, or metaphor that conveys your vision? Write or draw something in the space below that is inspired by God's knowledge and compassion.

PART 5
i am confident

I AM CONFIDENT, SO I CHASE RADICAL HUMILITY. In a world obsessed with status, I welcome humility. Does this make me insignificant? No. In fact, it's quite the opposite. It makes me teachable. It makes me capable. It makes me significant. And I use my significance—which cannot be shaken by position, season, or failure—for the purpose of service. Jesus—the greatest ever—modeled a new type of humility, humbling himself even to death on the cross. It's in his example that I find the courage to step into a supernatural confidence. I am confident, so I chase radical humility.

DAY 24

GOD IS AWESOME,
so i am humble

REST

Imagine yourself in the presence of God: his glory, his greatness, his love. Let yourself be in awe of him. Don't be afraid, don't be ashamed. He loves you immeasurably.

Take a couple of minutes to rest in his power and love. When you are ready, repeat to yourself, *I know who God is, so I know who I am. I am humble and confident in him.*

READ

Small but Mighty   There is something about sleeping under the stars that inspires awe. It can also inspire itching, depending on the local mosquito population. But assuming you thought to pack mosquito spray, a pitch-black night sky with the Milky Way in full view is nothing short of breath-taking. It makes you feel tiny, and at the same time it brings you closer to God.

If camping isn't your thing, there are other wonders that have the same effect. Trees changing colors in the fall, for example. Sunsets at the beach. A baby grasping your finger. Parallel parking on the first try. The list is endless. You could probably come up with a dozen things right now that remind you how big the world is, how creative God is, and how small you are.

David knew what it felt like to be small in the presence of an awesome God. He wrote, "When I consider your heavens, the work of your fingers, the moon and the stars, which you have set in place, what is mankind that you are mindful of them, human beings that you care for them?" (Ps. 8:3–4)

David recognized three things in these two verses. First, how great creation (and therefore God) is. Second, how small humans are. And third, how incredible it is that such a big God would care for such small people. That last realization was what most inspired his wonder and gratitude.

Small is not an insult. It's not demeaning. Small is an accurate description of human beings compared to God and the universe. In light of the infinite power, wisdom, and presence of God, we are tiny.

But being small does not mean we are insignificant. That's an important point. God created us in his image, after all. We can't replace him or compete with him, but we do *reflect* him. Not only that, but we are also *loved* by him, *empowered* by him, and *called* by him. We have a role to play in his plan. We might be small, but we are powerful, and we make our presence known. Like mosquitos, actually. But in a good way.

David found humility in God's greatness, and that humility gave him confidence. Not a confidence based on arrogance or self-promotion, but confidence that flowed from God's care and calling for him.

Sometimes we think humility means talking badly about ourselves or refusing to accept compliments or never doing bold things. We confuse humility with self-rejection. In reality, humility actually looks more like confidence than anything else.

Humility is not self-rejection, but self-acceptance. It's cultivating a view of ourselves that flows from God himself. Humility means having an accurate view of who we are. Not more, not less. It means accepting that what God says about us is true, even if we don't feel it or see it.

What does God say about you? Every chapter of this book helps fill in that blank, but ultimately this is a question for you to answer. As you get to know an awesome God—with his limitless power, infinite love, and amazing grace—pay attention to the value and calling he is giving *you*.

Be astonished by the stars and be encouraged. Let the greatness of God amaze you, and let it give you confidence. The same God who hung those stars in the heavens is caring for your needs and calling you to greatness.

For further thought, read Job 42:1–6 and Hebrews 12:28.

REFLECT

1. What is the most awe-inspiring part of creation? What is the most awe-inspiring thing about God?

2. Would you say you are a humbly confident person? Why or why not?

3. How does God's awesomeness inspire confident humility?

respond

Think about God's greatness and your place in the universe he created, then use the space below to illustrate your perspective of these truths. Use words, a sketch, a poem, abstract art, or anything else that gets your thoughts and feelings onto paper.

GOD IS PRESENT,
so i am not alone

REST

Quiet your thoughts and focus on God. Block out the busyness of the day ahead of you (or behind you). Be still.

Breathe slowly, rhythmically, deliberately. After a couple of minutes of stillness, whisper, *God is with me. No matter where I go or what happens, I am safe in his presence.*

READ

With You and For You   Imagine you are walking late at night in an unfamiliar part of town. Overhead a few dingy streetlamps create more shadows than light. The streets are deserted at this hour. You are completely alone, and you feel unsafe and unprotected. Subconsciously you lower your head and walk faster.

Now imagine that a car drives by on the other side of the street. It goes past you, stops, then turns around and comes back your way. As it pulls up next to you, the window begins to roll down.

What would you feel? Most of us would probably be terrified, and with good reason. The only thing scarier than being alone is being joined by someone who might mean to cause you harm.

The window rolls all the way down. A head pops out, and you recognize the driver's smiling face. It's on old friend from school, someone you trust completely, who happened to recognize you and is stopping to offer you a ride.

As you climb into the car, what do you feel? A rush of relief, probably. Maybe a little embarrassment over letting yourself get so freaked out. At the sight of your friend's face, you went from panic to peace, from feeling unprotected to feeling safe. Not only are you no longer alone, you are now joined by someone who is able to take you where you need to go.

In the same way, the presence of God brings us relief, peace, and protection. Because God is always present, we are never alone. And not only that. God takes us where we need to go and he protects us along the way.

Before he returned to heaven, Jesus knew his disciples needed reassurance of this. One of the last things he said to them was this: "Surely I am with you always, to the very end of the age" (Matt. 28:20).

The disciples took that promise seriously. Their lives were marked by courage. They were transformed not just by the teachings and the example of Jesus but also by his ongoing presence through the Holy Spirit. The book of Acts records story after story of how Peter, John, and other followers of Jesus were empowered to face even the most difficult circumstances.

As we've noted earlier, God's presence and protection doesn't mean life is easy and problem free. As a matter of fact, sometimes following God will lead us through rather scary scenarios. The promise is not that we will never face risk, pain, or loss but that God will go through every trial with us. His presence makes all the difference.

In a world that can often feel lonely and threatening, we can take Jesus's words to heart: "I am with you always, to the very end of the age." Jesus is the friend who comes alongside us when we are afraid and offers us protection, companionship, and direction. No matter the road we take, we are never alone.

For further thought, read Psalm 46:1–11 and Acts 1:8.

REFLECT

1. Do you feel alone, either in general or in a particular area? If so, how does that affect you? How do you deal with it?

2. Can you think of any practical ways you could become more aware of God's presence?

3. Does having God in your life make you braver? Why or why not?

respond

Use the space provided to illustrate, in whatever creative way you prefer, the idea that God is always with you.

GOD IS ETERNAL,
so i am patient

REST

Before you begin, take a moment to evaluate yourself. How are you feeling? Are you worried, tired, afraid, angry, sad?

Lean into the reality of God's care for you. Cast your cares on him, and let stress give way to the simple freedom found in Jesus.

Say to yourself, *God knows my needs. I am confident, I am patient, and I am secure.*

READ

Right on Time   Time travel has always been a favorite theme of science fiction and superhero movies. Famous movie franchises from *Back to the Future* to the *X-Men* series have story lines built around being able to manipulate time.

The appeal is obvious. Who wouldn't want to go back in time to fix a mistake? Or travel into the future and figure out winning lottery numbers? The ever-present plot hole, though, is what happens if you change something. Because in theory, if a problem existed that you wanted to fix, and you traveled in time to tweak whatever needed tweaked, then when you returned, the new version of reality wouldn't need tweaking anymore. It's fixed now. But since this new version of you now won't time travel to fix anything, the original problem will exist, after all, so you *will* have to time travel to fix it . . . It's a never-ending paradox.

Confused? Join the club. It's a mess. Good thing time travel only exists in movies.

Outside of movie characters (and the screenwriters who make them up), the only being not bound to the constraints of forward-moving time is God. God is eternal. He always existed and always will exist. In addition, he exists outside of time. He sees the past, present, and future.

Now, whether God is bouncing around on parallel timelines or spinning alternate universes into existence in his spare time is beyond us. What is very much within our grasp, though, is the fact that God's *timelessness* means we don't have to stress out quite so much about the *passage of time*. For example, how long it's taking to achieve that goal, find that spouse, build that career, or beat that level on Candy Crush. As a matter of fact, when we ponder eternity, our impatience over things that take a few days, weeks, or years longer than expected seems a bit illogical.

Since God's perspective is eternal, he can afford to be incredibly patient. If he can be patient, so can we.

Peter wrote,

> But do not forget this one thing, dear friends: With the Lord a day is like a thousand years, and a thousand years are like a day. The Lord is not slow in keeping his promise, as some understand slowness. Instead he is patient with you, not wanting anyone to perish, but everyone to come to repentance. (2 Pet. 3:8–9)

Peter was saying that what seems slow to us is right on schedule for God. He knows exactly what needs to be done and when to do it.

That should give us a deep sense of peace, especially when time seems a little out of control. Sometimes things will take longer than we expect. Other times, they'll come so fast and furious that we will feel perpetually behind schedule. Either way, dealing with time can be difficult for us.

Not for God though. He doesn't have time management issues. He doesn't procrastinate and he doesn't rush. He is never early and never late. He doesn't overbook or overcommit himself. He's not stressed out, behind schedule, or under pressure. His plans are perfect, his timing impeccable.

When David's life was threatened by enemies, he wrote, "But I trust in you, LORD; I say, 'You are my God.' My times are in your hands" (Ps. 31:14–15). He couldn't see the outcome of his current situation, but he was able to trust that his destiny was safe in God's hands. God's eternal perspective was the source of David's present peace.

The same truth can bring you peace today, especially if you are in a season of waiting. You aren't a member of the X-Men. You can't see the future, and you can't change the past. But you can trust in an eternal God, a timeless God, the Creator and keeper of time itself. He knows what you need, and he will always be there for you—right on time.

For further thought, read Psalm 139:16; Proverbs 16:32; and Romans 12:12.

REFLECT

1. Is it difficult for you to imagine an eternal God? Why or why not?

2. What does God's eternal perspective and presence mean for your day-to-day existence?

3. Are there areas where you feel you need an extra dose of patience today?

respond

Think about God's eternal nature and the place you occupy in time. What does eternity mean to you? What does patience look like? Use the space below to describe creatively how you envision these truths.

GOD IS INTENTIONAL,
so i am persistent

REST

Calm your mind. Don't say anything. Just wait.

If you have any worries, fears, deadlines, or pain points that are distracting you, consciously give those things to God. Let his peace fill you. Let him take charge of your life.

When you are finished, whisper to yourself, *I am confident in God's love and secure in his calling. The future is good.*

READ

Some Assembly Required   There is a particular rite of passage in adulthood that is responsible for more mental anguish, tears, and colorful words than maybe any other: assembling prefabricated furniture. If you know, you know.

Maybe you went to IKEA and found the perfect bookshelf or table for your apartment. But when you bought it, you realized it was packaged in a long, flat box that somehow must transform into a three-dimensional object. How? Well, as the box cheerfully states, "Some assembly is required."

So you pull out whatever tools you have and dive into the project. *How hard can it be?* you ask yourself. Famous last words.

Maybe you're the type who reads instructions, or maybe you're the type who figures it out on your own. That's between you, God, and IKEA.

Regardless of our furniture-assembling styles, we all share a basic assumption: the designers were *intentional* in their creation. Every screw and bolt should have a purpose. Every piece should fit together. Every page of the manual should follow a logical order. *The product was designed to be assembled by newbies*, we tell ourselves, *so this should work.*

Sometimes it does, and sometimes it doesn't. Sometimes there are random pieces of hardware left over. Sometimes little wooden pegs don't fit in the pre-drilled holes. Sometimes the pictures in the manual are less intelligible than ancient hieroglyphics. Sometimes you realize on step 74 that you installed a piece upside down on step 3, and you have to start over. But you persist, because you're an adult, and that's what adults do.

As you've likely guessed, this is a metaphor for life—including the anguish, tears, and colorful words. Often we have a mental image of what our life should look like, but let's be honest, it can be really hard to get there. Things don't always work out right. The pieces don't fit. We make mistakes and have to start over. Whether it's our romantic life, finances, career, relationship with our parents, or something else, we can find ourselves wondering how in the world we are supposed to make this work.

That's where faith in the Designer comes in. Our lives are not a bunch of random screws, bolts, and pieces of wood. Rather, we were designed and created by an intentional God, a God with a plan, a God who knows exactly what he is doing.

By the way, we are *not* mass-produced, prefabricated copies of each other—that's where this metaphor breaks down. Instead, we are intricately designed works of art. God's design for his children is unique, perfect, and beautiful.

When life feels a little random, or when pieces don't seem to fit, remember that God is intentional in all he does. That includes both how he designed us as individuals and what our future has in store. It might not make sense in the moment, but life is long, even longer than our time on earth, and there are a lot of things that still have to come together.

Paul famously wrote, "And we know that in all things God works for the good of those who love him, who have been called according to his purpose" (Rom. 8:28). That is one of the most encouraging verses in the Bible. It reminds us that God takes the things that make the least sense and uses them to create masterpieces out of our lives.

There's one more place where the metaphor breaks down: our Designer is helping us with the assembly. Yes, he lets us do a lot of the work ourselves. That's called autonomy, or free will, and it's a good thing. But we are never alone in the process.

If your current reality seems a long way from the dream in your head, be patient. Trust in the Designer. And yes, persist and persevere because the process might take a while. That's okay. God's designs always make sense in the end.

For further thought, read Esther 4:14 and Jeremiah 29:11.

REFLECT

1. Do you feel lost or confused in any area of life? How are you responding?

2. Is it hard for you to believe that God intentionally designed you the way you are? Why or why not?

3. Do you need to be more persistent and patient? In what ways?

respond

Think of a creative way to illustrate God's intentionality when he designed you. You might want to draw or write a poem or tell a story or jot down a few thoughts. It's up to you.

GOD IS HOPE,
so i am optimistic

REST

Before you begin reading, take a couple of minutes to breathe calmly and rhythmically until you are at peace. There's no hurry right now. No urgency or pressure.

When you are ready, tell yourself, *God is hope, and I am confident in him. My past, present, and future are in his hands.*

READ

All the Feels   Have you ever met someone who is a little *too* positive? As in Ted Lasso-level positive. Or SpongeBob-, Olaf from *Frozen*-, or Dory in *Finding Nemo*-level positive. You know the type: life is good, everything is amazing, and negativity is not allowed.

For the most part, those people are great to be around, even if their outlook can be a little exhausting at times. At least, it's preferable to the other extreme—eternal negativity. You know that type too: the Squidwards and Eeyores.

Most of us embody a little bit of both extremes, if we're being honest. Our precise emotional response at any given moment is not 100 percent positive or negative. Rather, it depends on the circumstances we face, our current mental state, and whether we've had coffee yet.

That's okay. It's normal. Moods are exactly that—moods. They go up and down like elevators. Insisting on absolute positivity can actually be a toxic habit because life has sad moments, not just happy ones. We shouldn't be afraid of recognizing loss, fear, failure, betrayal, or other difficult things we experience. They are part of being human, and the Bible doesn't shy away from these moments.

What we find in the Bible is not toxic positivity, but *hope*. Hope falls somewhere between wanting something to happen and expecting it to happen. It's a holy confidence that what the *good* God has placed in our hearts will become reality. We might not know the details (the when, where, and how), but we do know *God*. And because of our relationship with him, we have a calm assurance that the future is good.

Paul, writing to the Romans, calls God a "God of hope." Here's how he put it: "May the God of hope fill you with all joy and peace as you trust in him, so that you may overflow with hope by the power of the Holy Spirit" (15:13).

Earlier in the same letter, Paul referred to salvation as hope: "For in this hope we were saved. But hope that is seen is no hope at all. Who hopes for what they already have? But if we hope for what we do not yet have, we wait for it patiently" (8:24–25). Was Paul saying that our salvation is up in the air? Not at all. Rather, he was emphasizing that we haven't seen the full realization of it yet, and it's in God's hands, not ours.

That's a good way of looking at hope, actually. Hope points toward the future, meaning we still haven't seen all the good we can expect. And hope rests on God, meaning our expectations flow from our knowledge of God's goodness, love, and generosity.

Hope works best when it's connected to God. No, we don't know the future. But we know that God is already aware of that future. We know he's caring for us in the present. We've seen his goodness in the past. So, while we can't guarantee that everything will be easy or go the way we think it should, we can still keep a bright outlook about the days ahead.

Even when times are hard, we don't lose hope. If anything, our tears, sorrows, and struggles in those hard moments *prove* our hope. How? By validating the reality we are facing right now without giving up on our optimism for our future. It's not joy *or* sadness but both at the same time. We suffer *and* we have hope. We go through painful moments *and* we believe God has a future for us. We make mistakes *and* we are more than conquerors in Jesus.

You're not a one-dimensional movie character. You don't have to pick a personality. You're a human being—with all the complexities and nuances that identity entails—whose hope is in God. So be honest about what you're feeling, but don't deny God's grace, power, and love. It's in the tension that we discover what is most true about God and about us.

For further thought, read Genesis 50:15–21 and 1 John 3:2–3.

REFLECT

1. Do you tend to be more of an optimist or a pessimist? How is that working for you?

2. How could you improve at embracing the feelings of life without losing hope?

3. What are some things you are hoping for in the future?

respond

What does hope look like, feel like, or mean to you? Use the space provided to draw or write something that expresses how you view this concept.

PART 6
i am creative

I AM CREATIVE, SO I USE MY TALENTS TO REFLECT GOD'S GLORY. I was created for glory—a glory that mystifies the world's notion of grandeur. As a son or daughter, I participate in the wonder of new creation. I build for a beauty that has only been seen in parts. My Father is a creative God, and I share in his creative work. My brilliance is not used as a mechanism for self-promotion. Rather, I live in the awareness that I am a mirror, reflecting the glory of my Maker. I am creative, so I use my talents to reflect God's glory.

GOD IS DIVERSE,
so i am unique

REST

Take some time to quiet your mind, emotions, and body. Intentionally settle yourself. Let go of the tyranny of the urgent and the voices clamoring for attention in your mind.

Listen to the silence; become aware of God's quiet voice that speaks when you shut out external noise.

After a couple of minutes, remind yourself, *I am loved by God. I am unique and wonderful in his eyes—and in my eyes too.*

READ

The Many Ways to Be Human   In team sports, one of a coach's most important roles is to understand the needs of each *position* and the skills of each *player*, then figure out who to play in which position.

For example, if you're familiar with football, you know that a kicker and a lineman look massively different—like one hundred pounds different—and have completely different roles. One is in charge of kicking the ball and little else, while the other has to plow through half a ton of humanity on a regular basis. Imagine a lineman trying to kick a fifty-yard field goal or a kicker trying to protect the quarterback. It would make for a great meme, maybe, but a terrible game.

The same goes for just about any team sport. Think of a goalie versus a striker in soccer or a center versus a guard in basketball or a pitcher versus an outfielder in baseball.

The best teams aren't necessarily the ones with the best players—they are the ones with players who *work together the best*. The players must be good on their own, but individual skill isn't enough. Teams that figure out how to leverage each player's unique contributions toward a common goal are stronger than the sum of their parts. They are better together.

What does this have to do with you? Especially if you don't care about sports? Two things.

First, you should embrace the truth that diversity brings strength. That means valuing the differences in other people rather than criticizing them, rejecting them, mocking them, or trying to get them to change to be like you.

The diversity of humanity is a direct reflection of the diversity of God, after all, and God is infinitely creative. That means that as long as we live with love toward God and other people, there is no "right" or "wrong" way to be human. We have different gifts, tastes, philosophies, priorities, fears, hopes, dreams, abilities, and so much more. The possibilities and combinations are as endless as they are beautiful.

In the book of Revelation, John saw a vision of heaven that he described this way: "After this I looked, and there before me was a great multitude that no one could count, from every nation, tribe, people and language" (7:9). If heaven is that diverse, the world should be too, don't you think?

Mirroring the beauty of heaven starts with opening up *our* world. Rather than surrounding ourselves with people just like us, we need to diversify. We need to seek out, listen to, learn from, and celebrate people who are different.

That's not always easy, but it is necessary. *We need each other.* That was Paul's point when he compared diversity in the church to the different parts of the human body (see 1 Cor. 12). No member of the body can be strong alone. No member can say it doesn't need the others. And no member is worth more than any other, even if some parts get more praise than the rest.

Second, lean into the fact that *you* have a specific, important contribution to make (along with every human on earth). But in order to make your contribution, you have to be comfortable in your own skin. Too often, we spend a lot of time and energy trying to be like other people in order to fit in. Being socially aware is important, yes—but changing who you are to fit into some impossible, subjective mold is downright toxic. Imagine what would happen if, instead of stressing out over fitting in, you used that same time and energy to become the best version of yourself.

The world needs the real you, not the fake you. The fake you can't help anyone because by nature, it's not real. It's probably a copy of someone else, anyway. The world doesn't need two of anyone, but it does need *one* of everyone. Including you.

God designed the real you, and he did an awesome job. Lean into that truth. Own it. Love it. Accept and believe that your family, your church, your job, and your friends are all better off because you are here.

These two truths—that diversity brings strength and that you have a part to play—are connected. Diversity matters, so you matter. You matter, so diversity matters. They are two sides of the same coin, really.

So celebrate others and celebrate yourself. Let others be different and be different yourself. Then get out on the field with the rest of the team and play the game.

For further thought, read Romans 12:3–8 and 1 Corinthians 12:12–30.

REFLECT

1. Is it easy or difficult for you to celebrate who you are? Why?

2. How diverse is your friend group, workplace, or church? Is there any room for improvement?

3. Can you think of a specific instance when having a diverse team (in any area of life) added strength and creativity to the product, result, or experience?

respond

Use this space to express what diversity, uniqueness, and teamwork mean to you. You might pick just one of those concepts, or maybe you can think of a way to combine them all. As always, use whatever creative medium or expression fits you the best.

GOD IS UNPREDICTABLE,
so i am imaginative

REST

Imagine God filling you with warmth and peace. Open your heart and mind to his presence. Breathe out tension and anxiety. Breathe in God's love, joy, and creativity.

When you are finished, whisper to yourself, *I am full of God and full of life. I am creative, inspired, and imaginative.*

READ

Planned Spontaneity   There are two kinds of people: those who love routine and those who love spontaneity. And they sometimes marry each other. Or become roommates, at least.

Naturally, that leads to some drama. One person keeps lists, follows calendars, and arrives on time. The other loses every list they make, forgets to put things on calendars in the first place, and doesn't think in terms of "on time" or "late," but rather "going" or "not going." One person tends to worry about what might go wrong, the other enjoys what is currently going right.

Eventually, these types realize they need each other. That doesn't mean that the drama goes away, but the tension becomes meaningful because of what they receive from the other person, whether that's a little more routine in life or a bit of spontaneity. They figure out how to plan for spontaneity or add spontaneity to their plans.

God cannot be described as only spontaneous or organized. He can't be boxed into a personality type because he is all of them at once—all the positives without any of the negatives. However, from our perspective on earth, much of what he does is unpredictable. It can look to us like God is too spontaneous or he forgot his promises or he didn't plan for problems or he overlooked some important details. And naturally, that can cause some internal drama. Sometimes we wish he would just tell us the plan and then stick to that plan.

God is the greatest planner of all though. The fact that he is unpredictable *to us* doesn't mean he's disorganized or distracted. It can feel that way to us because he doesn't always meet our expectations or follow our timelines. Really, though, he has everything under control. The prophet Isaiah recorded God's words on the matter.

> "For my thoughts are not your thoughts,
>   neither are your ways my ways,"
>   declares the Lord.
> "As the heavens are higher than the earth,
>   so are my ways higher than your ways
>   and my thoughts than your thoughts." (55:8–9)

In other words, God has wonderful, wise plans, even when we don't understand what's going on. Sooner or later, it's all going to make sense, whether that's next month or in the age to come. Even in the craziest moments, we can trust that God's plans are good. Complex, nuanced, long-term, and beyond our full comprehension—but good.

Take this thought a bit further. If God is so good at thinking and planning outside of human expectations, it makes sense that we also should be remarkably creative. We were made in his image, after all, and we have a God-given ability to imagine the future and then work, plan, and pray toward that future.

Think about it. God could have listed every little thing out for us, like a detailed bedtime routine that a parent leaves for a babysitter. He could have organized and scheduled our lives so minutely that we would just have to check off boxes. How boring would that be though?

Instead, God has orchestrated an existence where we have vast ability to think, dream, and try new things. He is unpredictable, not just because his plans are higher than ours but also because he gives us a lot of leeway to throw our ideas into the mix. God wants to awaken our imaginations to participate in his plans. He wants to involve us, not control us.

We see this again and again in the Bible. People like Abraham, Moses, Elijah, and others didn't just robotically carry out orders; they interacted with God. They followed him, but they also suggested things to him. They listened to him, but they also shared their opinions and ideas.

This interactive partnership between humans and God is especially clear with Jesus and the men and women who followed him. Time after time, we see Jesus making plans but also being spontaneous when people had comments, questions, desires, or needs.

God is unpredictable. So is your spouse or your roommate. So are you. So is life. And that's okay. You weren't built just to check things off a list—you're too wonderful, too complex, and too creative for that.

When you don't know the plan, or when God doesn't seem to be sticking to your plan, learn to pivot. Use prayer and your God-given imagination to figure out what to do next. There's a lot to be said for plans, but there's a lot to be said for imagination and spontaneity too. Don't just be afraid of what could go wrong—learn to enjoy what's going right.

For further thought, read Proverbs 16:9; 19:21; and Isaiah 40:13–14.

REFLECT

1. Do you prefer routine, spontaneity, or something in the middle?

2. Is it hard for you to trust God when unexpected things happen? How do you usually respond?

3. What role does imagination play in your life?

respond

What does it look like to face an unpredictable world with a healthy, creative imagination? To follow an out-of-the-box God and to have some out-of-the-box ideas yourself? In the space below, express this concept of a divinely inspired imagination through whatever creative means you prefer.

GOD IS INFINITE,
so i am productive

REST

Take two minutes to focus on God's approval of you and his love toward you. You are all you need to be right now. Release insecurity, shame, and fear.

Say to yourself, *I am loved and called by God. My life has purpose, meaning, and direction in him.*

READ

Creativity Is Hard   Have you ever met someone who is a never-ending source of creativity? Every time you're around them, you are amazed by their ability to create new art, new music, new business ideas, new jokes, new stories, or new inventions.

It's like they have something inside them that can produce amazingness out of thin air. They see opportunities where others see nothing at all. They get inspired by the smallest, most insignificant things, then work their magic and generate something incredible.

It's easy to look at people like that and feel awe—and maybe a twinge of jealousy. Before you get too envious though, take a look in the mirror. *You* are that way too. Your creativity manifests in different ways than others, but it's no less creative.

Maybe you do something less stereotypically "creative," such as work on spreadsheets or financial systems. Maybe you create welcoming environments. Or friendships. Or reconciliation. Or you provide safe places for rescue animals, fashion treehouses, build furniture, make jokes. Or you . . . do something else. Your work may seem unimpressive to you, but if it creates value for others, it is, by definition, creative.

We usually don't impress ourselves because what we do seems so *normal* to us. It doesn't feel like awesomeness or amazingness. If anything, we are mostly aware of our deficiencies, our lack, and the mistakes we make. Someone comes along and tells us how great we did on a project or how impressed they are with our abilities, and we deflect. "It's nothing," we say. "Anybody could have done it."

But that's not true. We have been given a unique, valuable gift from God. It's the capacity to make something out of nothing. To take raw elements and create a finished product. To bring into existence what wasn't there before. To build, to do, to transform, to produce.

The author of Hebrews wrote, "By faith we understand that the universe was formed at God's command, so that what is seen was not made out of what was visible" (11:3). That's where creativity began. Literally, in the beginning.

Creativity doesn't just belong to God though. It is contained in the blueprint of humanity. In the Genesis account of creation, God told Adam and Eve to "be fruitful and increase in number; fill the earth and subdue it. Rule over the fish in the sea and the birds in the sky and over every living creature that moves on the ground" (1:28). Subduing and ruling here refer to leading, caretaking, and cultivating, not to abusing or destroying. God's heart for humanity is that we would be fruitful. That implies growth, productivity, and effectiveness.

Our work and diligence today are an extension of God's creative power. Only God can make *everything* out of nothing. He's the ultimate creator. But as humans made in his image, we can create *something* out of his everything.

Another word for this creation mandate, of course, is work. Not work in the sense of drudgery, but work in the sense of productivity. Note that

God created us with the capacity and calling to work in the garden of Eden, long *before* humanity fell into sin. Work isn't a curse or a result of sin. It's a blessing. It's the channel through which God continues to create.

Work can feel boring or insignificant at times, especially when we lose sight of what it's for. These lulls demand self-discipline and develop work ethic. Eventually, though, if we continue to show up, if we tune in to the creative spark inside us, we will build something beautiful.

Not just once either. We aren't one-hit wonders. We are a source of creativity that comes from God himself, and that creativity will continue to produce for as long as we put a demand on it. Our creativity doesn't run out because God's creativity doesn't run out, and neither do his resources. God is infinite, so we can be creative, fruitful, and productive.

For further thought, read Proverbs 10:4; 13:4; and Ecclesiastes 9:10.

REFLECT

1. How would you define the word *creative*?

2. What does creativity look like for you? How do you feel when you create something that you know is good?

3. Do you think you are productive and fruitful? In what ways? How could you be more productive?

respond

What does creativity look like, feel like, or sound like to you? What does it mean to be productive and creative with your time, talents, and passions? Use the space below to express your idea of creativity . . . creatively.

GOD IS MYSTERIOUS,
so i am curious

REST

Focus on bringing your mind to a place of peace and rest. Let go of hurry and worry, busyness and distractions.

Breathe in, breathe out. Feel where you are at. Love who God has made you to be. You don't have to be any more than that.

Tell yourself, *I am loved and called by God. Who I am is good, and who I am becoming is good.*

READ

The Joy of Chasing Rabbit Trails   Once upon a time, back in the olden days (aka the nineties), if you wanted to find the answer to an obscure question that popped into your brain, you had only one real option. Get in your car, drive to the library, find a book, magazine, or news article about the topic, and then start reading.

How exhausting. Now, thanks to the ever-expanding, always-helpful, often-snarky internet, the answers are literally at your fingertips. *Answers* might be too strong of a word because anybody and everybody can have an opinion online. Once you discard the sketchier sources, though, you can usually find what you're looking for. What's the life expectancy of a platypus? Seventeen years. Can you deep-fry a frozen turkey? Only if you want it to explode. How many McDonald's locations are there in the world? Thirty-seven thousand and counting.

The funny thing about human curiosity is that it's never satisfied. Sure, you discover the answer to your original question, but that only prompts three more questions. Soon you find yourself wandering rabbit trails, clicking links, and absorbing tidbits of random and probably useless knowledge—all while avoiding the work you're supposed to be doing. Then you have to rein in your curiosity, or at least direct it toward something more productive than figuring out how much you would weigh on Jupiter or whether armadillos are actually bulletproof.

Google might know a lot, but it's far from a comprehensive source for all knowledge—and it's definitely not infallible. God, on the other hand, knows everything perfectly, and his knowledge and wisdom are far beyond our understanding. There is an element of mystery to God that we will never fully resolve. In the book of Ecclesiastes, Solomon wrote, "He has made everything beautiful in its time. He has also set eternity in the human heart; yet no one can fathom what God has done from beginning to end" (3:11).

In other words, God is so far beyond us—so full of wisdom, understanding, and power—that he can be hard for us to figure out. Impossible, actually. He is mysterious, wondrous, awe-inspiring. Earlier we looked at Isaiah 55:9: "As the heavens are higher than the earth, so are my ways higher than your ways and my thoughts than your thoughts."

The mystery of God should do two things for us. First, it should inspire awe, humility, and trust. In the presence of God's infinite power, our smallness is more obvious than ever. Living grasped by the mystery of God is what Scripture calls the *fear of the Lord* or fearing God. This is a holy fear that fosters intimacy and safety. It woos us into wonder, beckoning us to run to God, not away from him, because there is no one and nothing beyond him. Holy fear also keeps us from reducing God to something we can manipulate and control for our own purposes. God created us in his image; we don't get to return the favor.

The second thing that God's mystery should inspire is a continual search to learn more about God and the world he created. It's no coincidence that humans are so curious. We were designed by God to learn, grow, explore, and change. There is an entire book of the Bible dedicated to learning— Proverbs. We are born knowing basically nothing, then we spend our entire lifetimes gaining understanding, knowledge, and wisdom. It's a beautiful process, driven by a mix of curiosity and necessity.

No, you'll never figure God out completely. Life either, for that matter. And that's okay. You can trust that you are safe in God's hands. But don't be surprised when you sense curiosity and hunger for learning grow inside you. Lean into your curiosity. Let it carry you closer to God. Let it push you to depend on God so you can walk in true wisdom and love.

Every random internet search is not the result of God stirring you— sometimes it's just your brain subconsciously avoiding work. But the drive to *learn* comes from him, and it's an awesome thing.

For further thought, read Proverbs 1:1-7 and Daniel 1:17-20.

REFLECT

1. What is the hardest thing for you to understand about God? About life?

2. How is fearing God different from being scared of God?

3. Why is the fear of the Lord the beginning of wisdom? How does it encourage curiosity?

respond

Take a few minutes to express creatively either the idea of God's mystery, your curiosity, or both. What do these things look and feel like to you?

GOD IS EXPANSIVE,
so i am intentional

REST

Consciously set aside your to-do list, your schedule, your phone. Just be alone with yourself and God.

Breathe in, then breathe out. Keep going until any tightness or tenseness evaporates.

Then tell yourself, *God's power fills me. His love flows through me. My gifts and creativity are precious, valuable, and needed.*

READ

Sky Full of Stars   If you look up at the night sky, the heavens seem pretty fixed and stable, don't they? You might see a few shooting stars, but other than that, most celestial objects follow patterns that can be predicted thousands of years in advance. That's why there are dozens of apps that can help you identify what stars or planets are overhead on any given day, from any given place.

Despite the still, peaceful appearance of the sky, literally everything we see is in motion. Not slow-motion either, but frantic, hyperbolic, mindblowingly fast motion. Stars, planets, the sun and moon, comets, galaxies—they are spinning, moving, and interacting on a scale that our brains can't comprehend. They don't appear to be doing anything from our perspective because they are so far away from us and from each other, but they are whirling and hurtling through space in a giant, cosmic dance.

That's not all. According to scientists, the universe itself is expanding, which means that everything is drifting farther and farther apart. That leads to the obvious question, *How will it all end?* There are many theories about the "end of everything," and most of them have names that sound like rides at an amusement park: the Big Rip, the Big Bounce, the Big Freeze, the Big Crunch.

None of them are very encouraging, to be honest. But since that is a good twenty billion years out (if it happens at all), you should still go to work tomorrow. The stars might be a few hundred miles farther away every second, but your office is right where it's always been.

The scale and movement of the universe is mind-boggling. It's beyond our comprehension. How much bigger, then, is the God who created it and set it in motion? One of the psalmists wrote this about God, "He determines the number of the stars and calls them each by name. Great is our Lord and mighty in power; his understanding has no limit" (147:4–5).

Our constantly expanding universe reflects the expansive, constantly-in-motion nature of God. He fills voids, like light filling darkness. Wherever he is, he expands to fill the space. Where there is need or lack, God is there. Where there is hate or evil, his love rushes in. He fills the universe, the earth, and our hearts. Just because God is unchanging doesn't mean he is immobile. Quite the opposite. He is always moving, always expanding, always loving.

You are expanding too. We all are. And that's not a reference to our waistlines. We should all be continually filling the spaces where God has planted us. Our abilities should be increasing, our love should be growing, our arms should be extending wider to bring more people close.

Solomon described this calling when he said, "The path of the righteous is like the morning sun, shining ever brighter till the full light of day" (Prov. 4:18). Imagine watching a sunrise. First you see a glow on the horizon. It's barely noticeable. Next a sliver of light peers above it, then the full disc of the sun appears, and eventually it burns high overhead, filling the world with light. That is a picture of the influence your life will have as God shines his love through you, extending his love outward.

God has called us to share in his expansiveness, and that means being *intentional* about how we live. We aren't shooting stars, burning up in the atmosphere. We are part of God's creation, set on a course by him, designed to accomplish good things, great things, generous things.

What does intentionality look like on a practical level? It might look like building a career. Or making art. Or getting a master's degree. Or loving your neighbor. Or composing music. Or getting married. Or having kids. Or staying single. Or starting a company. The possibilities are as countless as the stars themselves.

The point is to be intentional about using your life for *good*. To make a difference. To grow and to give, filling the spaces and places God sends you. This has nothing to do with being an extrovert, entrepreneur, or born leader. It has to do with your decision to make the most of your life.

No, you can't control what happens twenty billion years from now. But you can decide what to do *today*. And if you use every day for good, the trajectory of your life over time will be astounding.

For further thought, read Genesis 15:5–6 and Philippians 2:14–16.

REFLECT

1. Is it hard to believe that you could have a great impact in the world? Why or why not?

2. How do the greatness and goodness of God inspire you to make a difference?

3. In what ways could you be more intentional about doing good every day?

respond

What does God's expansive love look like? What does it mean to be intentional about doing good every day? Think about how you could express these concepts creatively, using the space below.

GOD IS DETAILED,
so i am excellent

REST

Take two minutes to center your thoughts and calm your mind. Be present. Relax. Smile. Breathe.

Let go of frustration over what you haven't accomplished yet or the things you still need to change. Enjoy who you are, where you are, all you are.

When you are ready, whisper to yourself, *God knows every detail of my life. I am full of his love, his joy, his creativity. He is enough for me, and I am enough for him.*

READ

Excellence Is Calling   Don't you hate it when you're taking a picture and suddenly your phone starts ringing? For most of us, the call function is one of the least-used aspects of our cell phones. Who makes calls anymore? They are an irritation, an interruption, a reminder that the real world exists and needs something from us.

The camera function, on the other hand, has never been more important. Detailed photos are a joy to view and share. Especially if you can zoom in on a friend's awkward expression and pass it around to your friend group. We want our cellular devices to take pictures in ever-higher resolution. To be able to zoom in on one thing and crop out the rest without losing quality.

To take pictures in low light or while moving or of objects far away. We want resolution measured in the millions of pixels per inch so we can take pictures with vibrant color and incredible detail. And we want telemarketers to stop interrupting our shot.

Details matter in everything, not just in photos. There is something beautiful about attention to detail. It's the details of a dress or coat that make it stand out in fashion. The details of a home remodel make us stop and admire each room. The details in artwork indicate the skill of its creator. The details in a story paint pictures in our minds.

When it comes to attention to detail, God is the master. He is the ultimate artist, skilled and excellent in all he does. Look through a microscope or a telescope or simply ponder nature, and you'll be amazed at the rich diversity and creativity of God.

In the creation story, we see God taking pride in his work. Multiple times during the creative process, God looked at his progress and saw that "it was good" (Gen. 1:10, 12, 18, 21, 25). When he was finished, Genesis records that "God saw all that he had made, and it was very good" (v. 31). In other words, it was something to be proud of and to celebrate. It was excellent, perfect, beautiful.

God is excellent, and he empowers us to embody that excellence. For example, he gave Moses detailed instructions about the place of worship he wanted the Israelites to build, and he also gave specific artisans the talent and grace to carry out those plans. God said this about a craftsman named Bezalel: "I have filled him with the Spirit of God, with wisdom, with understanding, with knowledge and with all kinds of skills—to make artistic designs for work in gold, silver and bronze, to cut and set stones, to work in wood, and to engage in all kinds of crafts" (Exod. 31:3–5). Then he added, "Also I have given ability to all the skilled workers to make everything I have commanded you" (v. 6). God anointed artists and creators of all kinds back then, and he anoints us today.

This isn't about pride, arrogance, or showing off. Paul, speaking specifically to servants or slaves (and by extension to anyone who works for a living) said, "Whatever you do, work at it with all your heart, as working for the Lord, not for human masters" (Col. 3:23). Notice how working with diligence and excellence is a form of worship. It's a way of pointing to God and giving back to him.

You can take pride in your work without being proud in your heart. There is a big difference between those two. Prideful people focus on being better than others; excellent people focus on being the best they can be. Prideful people use their work to bolster their ego and serve themselves; excellent people use their work to serve others. Pride is birthed out of comparison; excellence is birthed out of love—love for craft, love for truth, love for art, and most of all, love for people.

Only God can be perfect, but we can all be excellent. As a matter of fact, we were built for it. Just like that camera that keeps receiving calls.

For further thought, read Psalm 119:68 and Proverbs 22:29.

REFLECT

1. What does excellence mean to you?

2. What are you skilled at? What do you enjoy doing?

3. Do you struggle with diligence and excellence in your work? If so, what belief about yourself is informing this struggle?

respond

Can you express the concepts of excellence and attention to detail through words, poetry, a picture, or some other creative means? Illustrate what these ideas signify to you using the space below.

PART 7
i am called

I AM CALLED, SO I LIVE EACH DAY WITH PURPOSE. My life matters. Every day is energized with purpose. Each moment full of potential. God designed me on purpose, for a purpose, so I will not believe that my life is insignificant. Because of this, I invest in my character, calling, and community. I refuse to be stagnant, wasting away in self-pity. Purpose doesn't take a day off, so I won't be flippant with my time. I am called, so I live each day with purpose.

GOD IS SOVEREIGN,
so i am surrendered

REST

Breathe slowly for two minutes. Release anything that distracts you from the righteousness, peace, and joy that God freely gives you. Give it all to God. He can carry it better than you.

When you're ready, tell yourself, *God made me and chose me. I am surrendered to him. I am loved by him. I am called to greatness.*

READ

Giving Up Is Good   The word *surrender* means to submit voluntarily to a stronger force. If an army surrenders, it's because they lost the battle or war. If a soldier surrenders, they are taken into custody by the enemy. If a fugitive surrenders, they quit running and resign themselves to their fate. Examples like these are why surrender tends to get a bad rap—it is associated with losing or giving up.

Here's the thing though: surrendering is not always bad. It depends on what you are surrendering to and why you are surrendering. Every night you lie in bed, snuggle up under your blankets, and surrender to sleep. When a child relaxes in the arms of their parents, they surrender to the safety of people who care for them. When two people fall head over heels for each other, they surrender to love and to one another. If you bungee jump, skydive, or do some other activity that overrides the body's natural instinct to avoid falling from high places, you surrender to gravity, claiming the adrenaline rush is worth the terror. Maybe. Maybe not.

The point is, we can choose which "stronger force" to submit to, and if it's the right force, we benefit from it. We can give in to our passions and temptations or we can submit our wills to God's holiness. We can give in to fear and shame or we can surrender our emotions to God's peace. We can follow bad advice or we can surrender our choices to God's wisdom. The choice is ours, but the results are very different depending on what we choose. Paul, writing to the Romans, used the metaphor of slavery to highlight this choice.

> What then? Shall we sin because we are not under the law but under grace? By no means! Don't you know that when you offer yourselves to someone as obedient slaves, you are slaves of the one you obey—whether you are slaves to sin, which leads to death, or to obedience, which leads to righteousness? But thanks be to God that, though you used to be slaves to sin, you have come to obey from your heart the pattern of teaching that has now claimed your allegiance. You have been set free from sin and have become slaves to righteousness. (6:15–18)

Paul wasn't advocating slavery, of course, but he was using a culturally understood metaphor to remind us that we surrender to *something*, whether we realize it or not. We like to think we have total autonomy, but it's just not true. We are always influenced and led by forces around us.

If we don't submit to the higher power of God, we'll end up being controlled by our own passions, fears, and weaknesses. That's a terrible way to live because those forces are not on our side. They aren't watching out for us, they don't care about us, and they don't protect us. Ultimately they steal, kill, and destroy.

There is no one stronger or more loving than God, which means his arms are the safest place to be. His paths are the surest ways to walk. His will is the best choice for our lives. Surrendering doesn't undermine our autonomy, therefore, but rather empowers it, because God sets us free to be the best versions of ourselves. Plus, when we surrender to God, we discover a courage birthed from being on the winning side. We don't have to do everything on our own—we can lean on God, learn from him, and trust him to care for us.

Surrendering to God is a good thing. Like surrendering to sleep, we find rest in our heavenly Father. Like surrendering to a parent, we find safety in his arms. Like surrendering to love, we find unconditional commitment. Like bungee jumping or skydiving . . . well, we do find adventure in God. And in this case, the rush is definitely worth it.

For further thought, read Isaiah 45:5-7 and Romans 14:7-8.

REFLECT

1. What forces or voices, besides God, do you sometimes surrender to?

2. What benefits come from following God's will for your life?

3. Are there specific areas of your life that you need to surrender to God?

respond

Think for a moment about how powerful and good God is. What does surrendering to that power and goodness look like for you? Write or draw something that illustrates your life surrendered to God.

GOD IS MISSIONAL,
so i am ready

REST

Relax for a couple of minutes. Let tension and worry fall away as you lean into God. Simply be here, be yourself, without any expectations or demands.

Breathe regularly, slowly, intentionally.

When you are ready, repeat to yourself, *I am secure in God. I am safe in God's love and calling, and I am ready for whatever he has planned for my future.*

READ

Left On Read   There's a relatively modern social etiquette blunder we've all been the victim of—and probably inflicted upon a few friends as well. It's often called being *left on read.*

You know what this is. Maybe you are working on a project or have a question, so you reach out to a friend via text message, then wait for a reply. The little blue check mark shows up, and the word *Read.* So far, so good. They've seen your message. Maybe a few blinking bubbles even appear, indicating they are responding. You get your hopes up—it's going to be a quick reply and soon you can move forward with your plans.

Then crickets. Nothing. Not even a quick "I'll get back to you."

That's bad enough. Even worse is when you see them posting on social media a few minutes after that. *Are you serious?* you think. *They have time to doomscroll Instagram and repost cat videos, but they can't get back to me?*

It feels personal. Insulting. Humiliating. Until you remember you've done the exact same thing a few times. So you take a breath, forgive them, and write them back. And they usually respond as if nothing happened, unaware you've spent the last three hours questioning their loyalty, humanity, and character.

Why does it bother us that someone would see our question and not reply? First, because it keeps us from moving forward with whatever plan or project we are working on. Second, and more importantly, because it feels like they don't care about us. If cat videos hold more value than our friendship, we tell ourselves something is wrong.

Obviously there are multiple reasons a friend might leave us on read, or we might leave someone else on read, so we need to give each other the benefit of the doubt. Ask yourself though, *Do I ever do something similar to God? Do I ever forget to do something God has asked of me?* It might be a character issue you know you need to work on. It might be a person you feel prompted to reach out to. It might be a need in your world that you feel stirred up to meet.

James wrote this:

Do not merely listen to the word, and so deceive yourselves. Do what it says. Anyone who listens to the word but does not do what it says is like someone who looks at his face in a mirror and, after looking at himself, goes away and immediately forgets what he looks like. But whoever looks intently into the perfect law that gives freedom, and continues in it—not forgetting what they have heard, but doing it—they will be blessed in what they do. (1:22–25)

One important note: this is not about self-condemnation. There will always be more to do than we have time, energy, or ability to accomplish, so don't turn this into another way to feel shame. There's already enough of that in life. We aren't saviors of the world—Jesus has that covered.

Rather, it's about being responsive or obedient to God. He's a *missional* God. He has plans, purposes, and projects, and we play a role in them. We have the ability and the privilege to participate with him in so many beautiful, exciting ways. We just have to make sure we aren't leaving him on read when he asks us to do something.

God is not as easily offended as we are, and he doesn't have to wonder what is distracting us because he knows exactly what we're doing. He probably likes cat videos too. But doing what he asks is the best way we can spend our time, so sooner is better than later.

Why? For the same two reasons we want our friend to respond. First, because God is waiting for us. He's patient, but he won't wait forever. Second, because our readiness and response say a lot about the value we place on our relationship. Responding to God indicates we love him and care about the things that are important to him. It is an act of respect and a form of worship.

The prophet Isaiah wrote about his own response to God's call: "Then I heard the voice of the Lord saying, 'Whom shall I send? And who will go for us?' And I said, 'Here am I. Send me!'" (6:8). God spoke, Isaiah responded, and together they embarked on a ministry that has never been forgotten.

God is on a mission, and you play a part in it. He'll reach out to you—so be ready to respond.

For further thought, read Matthew 7:24–27; 21:28–32.

REFLECT

1. What is God's mission in the world?

2. How does God call us into that mission? How does he let us know what we can do and how to do it?

3. Are there specific areas where you know God wants you to do something but you haven't obeyed yet?

respond

Think about what it means to be ready and responsive to God. Then, using the space below, write or draw something that illustrates your concept of this relationship with him.

GOD IS VISIONARY,
so i am involved

REST

Pause. Become aware of what you are feeling. Don't worry about solving problems right now. Just notice what is filling your mind or affecting your heart.

Breathe in, breathe out. Let the pressures and stress melt away. Allow God's peace and joy to grow within you.

After a couple of minutes, remind yourself, *God is good, life is good, and the future is good.*

READ

God Won't Ghost You   Have you ever felt used by someone? Not a great feeling, right?

Maybe a classmate was nice to you and you thought a real friendship was forming, but it turned out they just wanted you to help them with their classwork. Maybe a work acquaintance was suddenly friendly, but it was because they hoped you would help get them a promotion. Maybe someone you dated played with your emotions, took what they could get, then ghosted you.

We've probably all learned the hard way that there is a difference between being valued for what you can *give* versus who *you are*. Even in environments where what we give is the main point—in the workplace, for example, or on a sports team—we hope to be treated as a person first and as an employee or player second.

If we aren't careful, we can end up feeling like God is just using us. Why? First, because we know God is a visionary with divine plans and purposes: "The plans of the LORD stand firm forever, the purposes of his heart through all generations" (Ps. 33:11). Second, we know he gives us talents, gifts, and vision, and he calls us to participate in his plans.

All of that is awesome. God has a specific goal in mind, and he equips and calls us to join his vision. The problem arises when we assume our value comes from what we accomplish for God and we forget how much we mean to him.

To be used implies an impersonal, utilitarian, transactional arrangement: you are "just doing your job." And when that job is over, you are no longer needed and therefore no longer valuable. You might even be discarded in favor of someone else who can contribute more. That's not God's way at all.

The God we read about in Scripture, the God personified in Jesus, doesn't discard people. He doesn't move us around like chess pieces, sacrificing a few here and there to win the game. In the Bible, we see God caring deeply about people. Flawed, broken, weak people. People who, like us, had good days and bad days.

God doesn't *use* people in the negative sense of the word, but he does *involve* people. There's a big difference between those two.

To be involved is relational. We aren't just a tool in God's hands, but a part of his family. God's vision is similar to what a parent would have for their children: He sees the best in us, he knows what we are capable of, and he is excited about what we will accomplish. He cares about what we do because he first cares about us, rather than caring about us because of what we can do. The difference is huge.

To our heavenly Father, we aren't disposable, expendable, or forgettable. He's not a celestial boss who fires us when we are no longer needed or a coach who cuts us because a better player came along. He doesn't take what he can get and then ghost us. We are beloved children, and there's nothing we can do to deserve that honor.

As his children, though, he wants to involve us in the "family business" of loving and serving a hurting world. He sees the need around us, and he recognizes our potential, our hidden talents, and the opportunities we have to shine.

The apostle Paul wrote to the Ephesians, "For we are God's handiwork, created in Christ Jesus to do good works, which God prepared in advance for us to do" (2:10). Around the same time, he wrote to the Philippians, "For it is God who works in you to will and to act in order to fulfill his good purpose" (2:13).

In other words, we are called, commissioned, and empowered to partner with God in doing good works. God is committed to you as a person, *and* he's excited about what you will accomplish. You are valuable no matter what you do, *and* you are capable of doing incredible things. Both are true. And both are awesome.

For further thought, read Acts 16:6–10 and 1 Corinthians 3:5–9.

REFLECT

1. Is it hard to believe that you are valuable to God regardless of what you do or don't do? Why or why not?

2. What does it mean to you to know that God is a visionary God? What does he see or envision?

3. What do you think God has specifically called you to do in this season with your gifts, talents, and time?

respond

Think about God's vision for the world and the important role you play in it. Use the space provided to illustrate this relationship, using whatever creative means suits you the most.

GOD IS FAITHFUL,
so i am strong

REST

Settle your mind and heart for a few minutes. If it's helpful, use breathing techniques to slow down.

Let God's peace fill you. If you are anxious or stressed, surrender those things to him and find rest for your soul.

When you're ready to continue, breathe out, *I am strong in God. I have gifts, I have a calling, and I have a future.*

READ

Casually Carving Canyons If you've ever been to the Grand Canyon, you probably stood in awe at its size and scale. It's over a mile deep, ten miles across on average, and nearly three hundred miles long. The formation of this canyon is just as amazing as its immensity. It wasn't caused by a massive earthquake, the impact of an asteroid, or anything dramatic at all, but rather the slow, steady flow of the Colorado river that—over time—cut through solid rock.

Nature contains countless other examples of the sculpting power of water. Currents, drips, and waves of water can dissolve just about anything. Water carves underground caverns, forms stalactites, reshapes coastlines, erodes hillsides, carries sand and sediment, affects weather patterns, and much more.

Water isn't the only small-but-steady force that alters the planet. So do wind, gravity, heat, cold, vegetation, animals, and people. None of those forces are that massive in themselves, but over time, they have great power.

Just as these natural forces can have an outsized impact on our planet's topography over the course of time, so, too, the steady effort and energy of each of us can shape the world around us. We might feel weak and provide excuses—*I'm only human. What can one person do?*—but our small strength applied over time can accomplish great things. Proverbs 25:15 reflects this truth: "Through patience a ruler can be persuaded, and a gentle tongue can break a bone."

While one person might not have a lot of strength at a given moment, their work over a lifetime does. And many people working together have an even greater effect. We were put on this planet to make a difference, but that difference is usually the result of many small efforts combined, not one grand action.

Think of any large company—Amazon, Boeing, Disney, Apple, Sony, Volkswagen. They didn't grow famous overnight. Even if they grew relatively rapidly, they are still the result of innumerable tiny decisions, small sacrifices, and daily efforts by people who were relentlessly faithful to their product. Not over a week, month, or year, but over decades.

Faithfulness is what builds the future. Not just in business, but in any area: your family, your friendships, your ministry, your calling. When you put in the work, day in and day out, your efforts compound. They begin to build momentum, and they leave a mark on the world. You need other things as well—skills, knowledge, and teamwork, to name a few—but none of those will be enough to build something lasting if they are not sustained over time.

God, of course, is the ultimate example of faithfulness. He is constant and consistent. He never wavers or changes. The prophet Samuel said, "He who is the Glory of Israel does not lie or change his mind; for he is not a human being, that he should change his mind" (1 Sam. 15:29). God has all the power in the universe and does mighty miracles when he wants to, but most of the time, he seems to prefer to work slowly and steadily through us.

What does this mean for you? First, you can count on God's faithfulness even when you don't see dramatic results. He might be working slowly, but his work is as irresistible as a river carving a canyon out of rock.

Second, your strength is found in faithfulness. Even if you don't feel particularly powerful, you can be consistent. You can show up every day and do what you need to do. Whether that means being faithful in your family, your work, your studies, your prayer life, your finances, your time in Scripture, your mental health, or something else, it's worth it. You are making progress, no matter how slow it seems. Someday you'll look back and be amazed at the progress you've made.

Is there an area of your life where you've felt like wavering lately? Maybe you know you are doing what is right, but you wonder if your efforts matter or you worry your strength is too small. Don't give up—but don't try to fix it all in a day either. Be patient, steady, gentle. Gain your strength from God's faithfulness, and just do what you can each day.

Over time, your efforts are a lot more powerful than you realize.

For further thought, read Proverbs 20:6 and Revelation 3:7–11.

REFLECT

1. What does faithfulness mean to you? How are you being faithful in your life?

2. Is it difficult for you to remain faithful and consistent to what you know to be most important in your life? Why or why not?

3. Are there specific challenges where you need more of God's strength? How does his faithfulness encourage you?

respond

What do faithfulness and strength look like to you? Use the space below to write or draw something that illustrates the strength you receive from God's faithful presence.

GOD IS GOOD,
so i am generous

REST

Get comfortable and focus on relaxing for a couple of minutes. It's easier to connect with God if your mind is clear and peaceful.

Let go of the hurry and rush of the day. This is a safe place, a calm and restful space.

When you are ready, whisper, *God has been good to me. I am blessed, and my life is a blessing to others.*

READ

A Family Business   Have you ever experienced the bliss and freedom that come from spending someone else's money? With their full approval, of course. We're not talking about theft here.

For example, your employer gives you a company credit card and tasks you with buying new equipment, so you get to go on a fully funded shopping spree. Or you are told to take a prospective client out for dinner to the nicest steak house in town, paid for by your employer.

You don't have to worry about where the money is coming from or whether you can afford it—that's someone else's job. Yours is to spend the money . . . and spend it you will, happily and freely.

You don't get to keep the purchases, of course (other than the steak you ate). Plus, you probably have a budget to stick to, and you're expected to make wise choices. Those are important caveats here. You can't go too crazy or that magic piece of plastic will never be entrusted to you again. But those are just details. The joy is in the spending.

In this scenario, your literal job description is to spend money on behalf of someone else. The goal is to put that money to good use, knowing two things: spending money is part of making money and the money is not going to run out (at least, we hope not). In this case, refusing to spend money would be a negative, not a positive. Stinginess, fear, or greed would make you a worse employee, not a better one.

Now consider for a moment that God is the source of our blessings and the owner of all the resources in the world. In Psalm 24, David wrote, "The earth is the Lord's, and everything in it, the world, and all who live in it" (v. 1). He also said, "The eyes of all look to you, and you give them their food at the proper time. You open your hand and satisfy the desires of every living thing" (Ps. 145:15–16).

In the spending spree metaphor above, God is the owner and we are the staff. Like an employee who receives both a paycheck and an expense account, much of what God provides for us goes toward fulfilling our own needs, but some is destined for others. Of course, we are friends and children of God, not mere employees. You might say this is a *family* business. God asks us to use the resources we've received—which are ultimately his—in a wise and generous way in order to carry out his mission.

What is the "family business"? *Doing good.* God is a good God, and he cares about the whole world. He loves every person. His heart is to save, bless, heal, protect, deliver, comfort, feed, clothe, visit, hug, welcome, em-power, transform, forgive, restore, liberate, and love each of us. Doing good includes sharing the gospel, which is the good news that we are saved from our sin and reconciled to God through Jesus. But our generosity is not lim-ited to sharing our faith, and it might not even start with that.

Jesus said that when we serve and love "the least of these brothers and sisters of mine"—referring to people in need—we are doing it for him (Matt.

25:40). He told his disciples that rather than spending too much time and energy worrying about their basic needs like food, clothing, and shelter, they should seek God's kingdom: "For the pagan world runs after all such things, and your Father knows that you need them. But seek his kingdom, and these things will be given to you as well" (Luke 12:30–31). Jesus wasn't telling them to ignore responsibility, but rather reminding them that life is bigger than simply surviving and that God always provides for us.

There is great joy, promise, and freedom in generosity. Listen to how Paul described this kind of faith-based, God-inspired giving:

> Each of you should give what you have decided in your heart to give, not reluctantly or under compulsion, for God loves a cheerful giver. And God is able to bless you abundantly, so that in all things at all times, having all that you need, you will abound in every good work. (2 Cor. 9:7–8)

Everything comes from God, and everything belongs to God. He invites us to trust him, receive from him, and represent him everywhere we go.

How? By freely giving his goodness away.

For further thought, read Luke 12:22–34 and 2 Corinthians 9:6–15.

REFLECT

1. How have you experienced God's goodness and provision in the past?

2. How are you using the resources (time, money, energy, abilities, knowledge) that God has given you to help the family business?

3. If you had endless resources, what would you do to make the world a better place?

respond

Consider God's goodness and generosity for a moment. Can you think of a creative way to illustrate his giving and loving nature and the part you play in sharing his goodness with others?

GOD IS FIRST,
so i am fearless

REST

Take a couple of minutes to find rest in God's power. Relax in his arms of mercy and grace. Let God be God, so you can be you.

When you feel ready, whisper, *I am accepted and approved by God. I am called by love, with love, to love.*

READ

You Go First   Think of a time a sibling or friend tried to talk you into doing something you were both scared to do. Maybe it was jumping off a bridge into a lake or dealing with an enormous spider on the wall or talking to a group of cute girls or guys at a party or doing a polar plunge or trying a new dish in another country.

"Just do it," they told you. "It's easy. It'll be great. What do you have to lose?"

"Yeah?" you responded. "Okay, you go first, then."

If or when one of you got up the nerve to do it, the other probably followed. Why? Because it's easier to do something scary when you see someone you trust do it first.

Jesus doesn't ask us to do anything he hasn't already done. He isn't just our Lord and our Savior, he's also our example. He lived out in real time the qualities and actions that God asks of us.

Jesus was generous with his time and resources.

Jesus welcomed people who were different from him.

Jesus was patient and gentle.

Jesus didn't compromise.

Jesus served those around him.

Jesus forgave his enemies.

Jesus walked in the power of God.

Jesus lived in holiness and purity.

Jesus introduced people to God.

Jesus empowered those around him.

Jesus responded to opposition in both humility and boldness.

Jesus persevered until the end and obeyed God, no matter what.

Jesus loved God with all his heart, soul, mind, and strength.

Jesus loved other people as himself.

Jesus was the best example and the perfect model to follow. That's why Paul wrote, "Follow God's example, therefore, as dearly loved children and walk in the way of love, just as Christ loved us and gave himself up for us as a fragrant offering and sacrifice to God" (Eph. 5:1–2).

Jesus himself encouraged his followers to imitate and follow him many times. Matthew records him saying,

> Come to me, all you who are weary and burdened, and I will give you rest. Take my yoke upon you and learn from me, for I am gentle and humble in heart, and you will find rest for your souls. For my yoke is easy and my burden is light. (11:28–30)

Another time, Jesus told his disciples, "A new command I give you: Love one another. As I have loved you, so you must love one another. By this everyone will know that you are my disciples, if you love one another" (John 13:34–35).

God always goes first. He doesn't send us anywhere he wouldn't go, and he doesn't ask us to do anything he wouldn't do. When he tells us to love, it's because he loved. When he asks us to forgive, it's because he forgave. When he encourages us to be generous, it's because he gave everything.

As humans made in the image of God, we know that who we are reflects who God has always been. We look to him for leadership, inspiration, and wisdom to fulfill his purposes for us. We walk in confidence knowing that our Savior has *made* a way, and our Creator is *leading* the way.

We have not been left alone to wander unassisted through the labyrinth of life. Instead, we follow the lead of our Good Shepherd, who leads us to green pastures and quiet waters, who restores our soul and guides our paths, even when they lead through valleys of darkness and death. He goes with us and comforts us and provides for us (see Ps. 23).

God's presence and example calm our fears. He goes first, so we are fearless. Well, maybe not *completely* fearless, but at least confident enough to attempt some pretty amazing things. Remember Peter walking on the water? He *saw* Jesus, so he was inspired to *follow* Jesus—out of a boat, in a storm, over the waves. Even when he faltered, Jesus was there for him (see Matt. 14:25–32). In the same way, God helps our courage and faith grow the more we follow him.

Do you need courage? Look to Jesus. Consider his love, faith, and teachings. Then follow him wherever he leads you. He is always first and always faithful.

For further thought, read Psalm 23 and Hebrews 12:1–2.

REFLECT

1. Do you tend to struggle with fear or worry? If so, are there specific areas that are more challenging than others for you?

2. How do Jesus's example and presence help you deal with fear?

3. What are your dreams for the future? How could looking to Jesus help you address the fears, challenges, or obstacles you might face in pursuing those dreams?

respond

How does God's presence and example create a safe place for you to take risks and attempt great things? In the space below, use words, poetry, lyrics, or a picture to illustrate God's willingness to go first and your fearlessness to follow.

CONCLUSION

THANK YOU FOR JOINING US ON THIS FORTY-DAY EXPERIENCE. By now it's probably clear that one book can't possibly contain all of God's characteristics, nor the ways those characteristics are reflected in us. That's okay. This is only a beginning. You can spend the rest of your life getting to know God better and discovering the countless ways his image shines through you.

That discovery process is a very personal one. A devotional journey like this is a great place to start, but ultimately, your walk with God is *yours*. He wants to reveal himself to you more and more in ways that are specific to you.

Remember, God will never leave you, never forsake you, never reject you. That means you have nothing to fear or hide. You can come boldly before his presence any time, any place, any way you want. Like every good father would, God loves to be with his children.

As you follow him, you'll discover his righteousness, peace, and joy. You'll become more *you*, and you are who you most need to be. No, life won't always be easy. "Easy" isn't the goal anyway. It will be incredibly fulfilling, though, and anything but boring.

Now it's time to live out what you've learned here. Decide to follow Jesus—his example, his teachings, his invitation to live an abundant life. He was the best example ever of how to be human, after all. You are called and empowered to think like him, act like him, talk like him, laugh like him.

And most of all, love like him.

SONS & DAUGHTERS is an initiative that helps young adults discover the adventure, freedom, and purpose found in their Creator. Founded by the Beveres, what began in 2017 as a few YouTube videos for millennials has grown into a collection of studies, podcasts, events, and a global community with Ambassadors in over forty countries. For more information or to get involved, visit SonsAndDaughters.tv.

S&D

JOURNEY WITH US ON INSTAGRAM

@sonsanddaughterstv

Find community.

Grow spiritually.

Be encouraged.

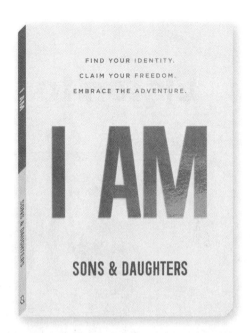
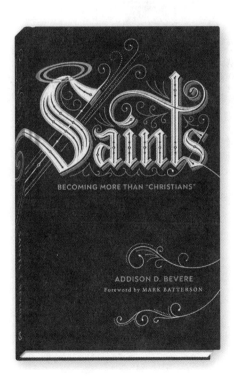

Listen to the Podcast

LET'S TALK ABOUT IT.

NAVIGATING HARD CONVERSATIONS

Tune in as we tackle today's hot topics and talk about how to navigate these hard conversations as sons & daughters of God.

sonsanddaughters.tv